Piano Lessons in the Grand Style

From the Golden Age of
The Etude Music Magazine
(1913–1940)

Edited and with an Introduction by
JEFFREY JOHNSON
Associate Professor of Music
University of Bridgeport

DOVER PUBLICATIONS, INC.
Mineola, New York

Bibliographical Note

This Dover edition, first published in 2003, is a new compilation of articles
originally prepared for *The Etude Music Magazine,* published by Theodore
Presser Co., Philadelphia, between 1913 and 1940. Dover Publications gratefully
acknowledges the cordial cooperation of Presser in making this edition possible.

Dr. Jeffrey Johnson, Associate Professor of Music at the University of
Bridgeport, Connecticut, conceived the idea for this publication, prepared an
introduction for the Dover edition, and compiled and edited all selected materials.
His clarifying commentary on the original lessons appears in square brackets
within the original texts; as needed, he scanned and electronically enhanced the
original music scores for clarity.

International Standard Book Number: 0-486-42424-3

Manufactured in the United States of America
Dover Publications, Inc., 31 East 2nd Street, Mineola, N.Y. 11501

CONTENTS

Introduction

Greatness in Art Cannot be Bought with Money

THE ETUDE has presented a wonderful series of master lessons like the foregoing . . . We have never represented that these lessons have been as good as lessons in person with the teacher. We know that they are not. Yet, it is a fact that many readers will gain more from such lessons than will many pupils of means and opportunity who can and do study with illustrious teachers. In reading the foregoing you will naturally miss the magnetic personality and the fine keyboard illustrations of such teachers as Sigismund Stojowski. Yet no teacher could give more details in a lesson, more direct help, more clear explanation than is given in the foregoing lesson[s]. These lessons present a real opportunity to students who are denied the privilege of studying with master teachers, not merely because such teachers charge ten or more dollars a lesson, but because there never will be enough men at the top to accommodate all those who need such expert advice.

[ETUDE, January 1915].

The Etude Music Magazine forged an American musical community on a scale never before accomplished, as a monthly publication spanning the years 1883 through 1957. The creative energy behind the magazine radiated from Theodore Presser (1848-1925) who began its publication at age 35. According to the "Thirty-Year Jubilee of THE ETUDE" in 1913, Presser "resigned a profitable position [as professor of piano and music theory at Hollins College, Virginia,] and with a ridiculously small capital [$250] he started THE ETUDE. Eight months after the founding in Lynchburg, the office was moved to a little third-story back room [on] Walnut Street, Philadelphia." In radical expansion, several quick moves found the offices located in three buildings with 40,000 square feet of office space on Chestnut street. "The bill for postage alone during [1912] exceeded $75,000. Indeed, a large new branch U.S. Post Office ha[d] been erected in the vicinity of the Presser building, principally because of the vast increase in the Presser business."

THE ETUDE connected local communities with the most respected pianists of the time, and was also a creative outlet for its subscribers. Every issue abounded with pedagogical articles, tips and advice on playing, teaching, and musical repertoire at all levels. The repertoire included new original compositions, from emerging composers and neighborhood musicians, sent in from all over the country. As quality varies dramatically, the deeper value of these articles and compositions are often not revealed in random quick perusals. Taken as a whole, they read like a diary of an emerging American musical tradition.

In the midst of this cultural diary, THE ETUDE wove a long series of what they termed "Master-Lessons" by "Noted" or "Famous" virtuosi. The original intention of this extremely popular series was practical, providing pedagogical advice from world-class pianists on a specific piece, with an annotated edition included for direct study. It is evident that these lessons were also models for teaching; to help set standards for excellence and to supply uniquely *applied* resources.

What was also created, perhaps unintentionally, was an invaluable record of performance practice and piano pedagogy as it existed, transformed from the orality in which it was normally generated and transmitted from teacher to student during lessons. The written piano lesson is an idealized model of both teaching and learning; but it allows us to observe and experience something of a process normally lost.

Preferences in format and style changed during the time span of these lessons. Basic issues pertaining to the balance between emotional essences and historical contexts relevant to the work, and balances among objective technical information, advice and description shift quite perceptibly.

The first published lesson appeared in the January 1913 issue. It was called an "Analytical Lesson" on the Anton Rubinstein *Barcarolle* in F minor, and yet Sigismund Stojowski opens the lesson with a dream vision. In it he sees Rubinstein's face, and a direct connection, passing from the generation that knew Rubinstein to the younger generation that did not. This is what Stojowski seeks to communicate

as he begins to "collect his humble wits," and write. This lesson served to set the standard for later lessons. The potential of this new format—imaginative, yet weaving descriptive details into explanations based both on emotional and analytical platforms—is made manifest. The "undercurrent of melancholy and pathos, suggestive of individual emotion and northern skies" is articulated, but also the musical structure and harmonic planning, where the high $A\flat$ in measure 14 is understood within the shifting harmonic context and architecture of the phrase and described as "a surprise." This important quality can only be properly felt when a sense of expectation has been created and altered, and Stojowski provides students a chance to sensitize to this context, and to shape the hands and wrists, using every means to craft the emerging envelope of the phrase. Guiding explanations, both technical and emotional, transmit a sense of authority to his descriptions.

The death of Theodore Presser in 1925 marked a new generation in The Etude Music Magazine. It is also marked a new generation of Master Lessons with the model established and perfected by Mark Hambourg. His first, written in 1926 on the Liszt *Liebestraum* No. 3, opens with historical context, and instructions for the emotional framework are presented, but these emotions are derived from the poem rather directly, not invented afresh by Hambourg. "An intense feeling tinged with melancholy" evokes Stojowski and the earlier style, but Hambourg is at home when he is reveling in musical details that are not abstract emotions but directly under the fingers. "The arpeggio-like accompaniment . . . should be played throughout with a juicy tone, not only as a mere figure but as a sensuous adjunct to the melody." This incredibly vivid description seems immediately compelling and useful, and Hambourg suspects that no additional explanation for his interpretation need be advanced. Strongly subjective readings are often encased in technical details and directions resplendent and memorable, and become more so in later lessons as Hambourg got comfortable with a new medium that he developed with unique personality.

The master-lesson series was an instant success and ran to the very end of The Etude Music Magazine in 1957, with the last installment in the second-to-last issue. The forty-year span included just short of 100 lessons, roughly divided in half from 1913-1930, and 1931-1957.

In my personal copy of the June 1912 ETUDE , there are numerous pencil markings. Ruth Pieney read through almost every piece in the issue, marking fingerings, and noting interesting and unexpected harmonies with little arrows. It is one of many issues given to me by my mother, who as an antique dealer regularly came across them, and brought them home for me. Remembering this fondly in the Fall of 2000, I purchased more than 650 issues, and little stacks of "Etudes" have literally covered all open spaces in my office and home. The process of reading and absorbing them has been enlightening in ways even beyond my expectations. The master-lesson series illuminates an extraordinary fellowship with the past.

Jeffrey Johnson
New York City
June, 2002

Pianists in this Edition in Contemporary Accounts

Wilhelm Bachaus [1884-1969]

"Wilhelm Bachaus, born at Leipzig, March the 26th, 1884, is a pupil of Alois Reckendorf, a Moravian teacher, who was a professor of pianoforte playing at the Leipzig Conservatory for some thirty years. This unusual master had been a student of science and philosophy at the Vienna and at the Heidelberg Universities and was well known as a musical savant. He identified the keyboard genius of Bachaus and left nothing undone to develop his great talent. Thereafter Bachaus spent a year with [Eugène] d'Albert [1864-1932] and later had a few lessons with [Alexander] Siloti [1863-1945]. Although he appeared publicly at the age of eight, his real début did not occur until 1901. In 1905, he won the Rubinstein Prize at Paris, one of the great distinctions of the pianistic world. His public appearances in Europe revealed intellectual and emotional power of the loftiest order accompanied by one of the most astonishing technical equipments ever possessed by a pianist. His tours of America have been extraordinarily successful. His playing of Beethoven has brought him international fame as a Beethoven interpreter. This is the result of the most exhaustive study of all the details of the performance of the works of the great master." [ETUDE, October 1926].

Victor Biart [1878-1952]

"Mr. Biart is a brilliant pianist and a very interesting lecturer. For a time he was the official lecturer of the New York Philharmonic Orchestra. He was a pupil of Dionys Pruckner [1834-1896] at the Stuttgart Conservatory. He has toured Germany and Belgium, as well as America, as a pianist." [ETUDE, August 1925]. "Norwalk, Conn., March 26 [1952]. Prof. Victor Biart, musician and conductor, died early today in the Norwalk General Hospital after a brief illness. He was 75 years old. His home was at 34 East Avenue here." [NYT, Mr 27, 1952, 29:4].

Cécile Chaminade [1857-1944]

"Mme. Cécile Chaminade, the author of the following article, is without doubt the most successful of all woman composers. Her compositions have sold enormously in all countries where the pianoforte is popular. She rarely writes for publication, and we feel that our readers, to whom an article of this kind must be of great usefulness, will join us in our thanks for her time and attention taken in preparing this article expressly for us. Mme. Chaminade's great popularity is shown by the fact that two weeks before her arrival in this country every seat for her first concert at Carnegie Hall was sold." [ETUDE, December 1908. Another general article: *Recollections of My Musical Childhood* appears in the December 1911 issue.]

Maurice Dumesnil [1886-1974]

"Eminent French concert pianist. Studied at Paris Conservatory under Isidor Philipp. Successful tours of Europe and America. Educational articles in magazines including THE ETUDE." [ETUDE, January 1933]. ". . . the distinguished French Virtuoso pianist, conductor, Debussy disciple and teacher, Member of the Piano Juries at the Paris Conservatory, The Ecole Normale and the American Conservatory at Fountainbleau." [ETUDE, March 1938]. [Author of *How to Play and Teach Debussy* (1932). *Claude Debussy; Master of Dreams.* (1940), and etc.]

Arthur Foote [1853-1937]

"The name of Arthur Foote has been carried, on the wings of song, to the farthermost corners of the earth. Before entering college he studied with Stephen A. Emery [1841-1891]. After matriculation he commenced the study of composition with John K. Paine [1839-1906]. Mr. Foote, immediately after graduation from Harvard University in 1874, in due course established himself as a piano instructor in Boston. He has been a prodigious worker. His output is enormous, and his pen is ever busy. The next ten years should give us many more fine works—if his life is spared—and it is safe to say that anything he produces will be a distinct and welcome addition to our musical literature. He married Miss Kate G. Knowlton July 7, 1880, and for quite a number of years lived in one of the quaint old homes on West Cedar Street. Of course, Foote, who is quite a club man, belonging to St. Botolph and Tavern Clubs in Boston, and Norfolk Golf Club in Dedham, has a very large acquaintance with professional people." [Wilber Hascael, from *Music News* ii/7 1909, p.18-20].

Percy Grainger [1882-1961]

"Percy Aldridge Grainger, whose compositions and pianoforte playing have won him international recognition as a genius, [was] born at [Melbourne], Australia, . . . was first trained by his mother, then Louis Pabst of Melbourne [during 1892], then six years with the great Dutch piano teacher J[ames] Kwast [1852-1927] of Frankfort, later, a short time with Busoni. He made his professional debut at London in 1900, when he was seventeen, commencing a long series of ovations which have attended his performances. As a composer he is largely self-taught. His early inclinations were toward the polyphony of Bach, but later he became greatly enamored of folksong and primitive music in general, making extensive investigations of all manner of folk and aboriginal songs, collecting some five hundred phonographic records of tunes from many different peoples. The combination of these two influences (of Bach and of folk-music) are chiefly accountable for the most salient characteristics of Grainger's creative 'style.' While he has employed many traditional melodies in his compositions, many of his own tunes, altogether original with him, have been so identified with the folksong genre that many have been deceived into believing that they were ancient ditties." [ETUDE, October 1921].

Mark Hambourg [1879-1960]

"Mark Hambourg, who is now twenty-six years old, is Russian by birth and parentage. When only eighteen months old he showed an interest in music, but it was not until he was six years of age that he gave evidence of talent and was put under regular instruction by his father, who is a teacher of great skill. The boy did not appreciate the opportunity; instead, he endeavored to run splinters into his fingers so as to get out of practicing. In 1888, Mr. Hambourg, senior, was appointed professor of piano playing at the Moscow Conservatory. Later, the family moved to London, where they now live. Mark Hambourg is now a naturalized Englishman. In 1892, he went to Vienna to study with Leschetizky [1830-1915]. Of his first experiences, he says:

"I went, and had a rude awakening. I had been thoroughly spoiled in England, and thought I knew everything. Leschetizky very soon showed me that I knew next to nothing. He was tremendously strict, and made one work desperately hard; but I have nothing except the kindest feeling for him, if at the time I often rebelled against his discipline. He was a very quick-tempered man, and most impatient of stupidity. One day, at our weekly concert, a student, who, like myself, thought he knew everything, was playing a piece very much to his own satisfaction, when the maestro, without a word, took him by the collar and flung him clean out of the room. It is only fair to that student to add that he is now a very distinguished and successful pianist. But Leschetizky had the kindest of hearts. When I was leaving him he called me into his room and said: 'Now, I have some money for you.' I was astonished for I could not think what he meant. 'All the money you have paid to me,' he continued, 'I have put aside for you, so that when you made your start you should not be hampered by lack of means.' However, as I had already secured an engagement, I did not need the money, so I did not take it, and the maestro characteristically gave it away to someone else." [ETUDE, Feb. 1906].

Clayton Johns [1857-1932]

"One of the most prolific and successful of American songwriters is Clayton Johns. His fertility is largely due, no doubt, to singleness of purpose, for, with the exception of a Berceuse and a Scherzino for the violin, which have been played by the Boston Symphony Orchestra, a chorus for women's voices with string orchestra, a few part-songs and a little music for violin or piano, Mr. Johns has devoted himself strictly to lyric expression.

He was born at New Castle, Delaware, November 24, 1857, of American parents. He first took up architecture as a profession, but gave it up for music. His American teachers were the brilliant critic, William F. Apthorp [1848-1913], John K. Paine [1839-1906], and the eminent native pianist, William H. Sherwood [1854-1911]. Mr. Johns then went abroad, and at Berlin studied under Kiel, Grabau, Reif and Franz Rummel [1853-1901]. Upon his return to America he took up his residence in Boston, and is a prominent factor in the musical life of that city." [from *Songs by Thirty Americans,* ed. Rupert Hughes, 1904].

In Memoriam Mrs. Edward MacDowell 1857-1956

"THE ETUDE joins with thousands in the music world who have paid tribute to the memory of the frail little lady with indomitable spirit—Mrs. [Marian Griswold Nevins] Edward MacDowell who died in Los Angeles, California, on August 24, just a few months under ninety-nine years of age. Widow of the first American composer to win international recognition, Mrs. MacDowell could have had a brilliant career of her own as a piano virtuoso. She chose rather to subordinate her own ambitions to the task of helping her struggling husband to attain fame and recognition as a composer, and then after his premature death, devoted herself to acquainting the world with his music, and later to the tremendous task of developing the MacDowell Colony in memory of her husband, where all workers in the creative arts might find encouragement and inspiration. Many world famous artists and writers, including Aaron Copland, Willa Cather, Thornton Wilder, Roy Harris, and Stephen Vincent Benet have sought the seclusion of the MacDowell Colony.

Mrs. Marian Nevins MacDowell was born in New York City November 22, 1857, and at an early age had her first music instruction from an aunt. Later she studied in Germany with Edward MacDowell whom she married in 1884. An indication of her unselfish devotion was her insistence that her husband use $5,000 which had been left to her for music study, for his own study as a composer. They finally were able to buy a farm in Peterborough, N. H. where later was located the MacDowell Colony.

Due to the ailments of advancing old age, Mrs. MacDowell was compelled to spend her last years in California, but before that she was a familiar figure on the 400-acre colony. She was loved by all who came in contact with her. Many tributes and awards were given to her in recognition of her devoted service, including the award from the National Institute of Arts and Letters in 1949, and the Henry Hadley Medal for outstanding service to music in 1941." [ETUDE, November 1956].

John Orth [1850-1932]

"John Orth enjoyed exceptional educational advantages in Germany where he was, during a period of five years, the pupil of Liszt, [Theodor] Kullak [1818-1882], [Ludwig] Deppe, Lebert, Faisst and Kiel. Since then he has taught in Boston for upwards of forty years, during which time many well known pianists have passed under his tuition." [ETUDE, May 1914].

Isidor Philipp [1863-1958]

"Isidor Philipp is one of the few living pupils of Stephen Heller [1813-1888]. He studied with him at a time when Heller's work was very widely recognized and he was in position to gain a comprehensive idea of his teacher's main characteristics as a pedagog." [ETUDE December 1912] [studied piano with Georges Mathias at the Paris Conservatory and later taught there from 1893-1934.] "Professor Philipp is making his first visit to America this year [1934, he moved to New York in 1941]...[he] is the chairman of the committee preparing the elaborate ceremonies for the one hundredth anniversary of the birth of Saint-Saëns next year." [ETUDE, July 1934]. "Nonagenarian: Isidor Philipp, at age 92, plays Franck Sonata at Carnegie Recital Hall today." [NYT, Mr 20, II, 7:7 1955]. "The mastery and wisdom of his years and his passion for the music were notably communicated." [NYT, Mr 21, 21:3 1955].

Sigismund [Zygmunt] Stojowski [1869-1946]

"Sigismund Stojowski was born at Strzelce, Poland, [May 14, 1869]. He studied piano with L. Zelenski [1837-1921] at Krakow and with Diémer at the Paris Conservatory. At the same institution, he studied composition with [Léo] Delibes [1836-1891]. His talent both as a composer and as a pianist, [was] considered extraordinary at that time, and he was successful in carrying off two first prizes, one for piano playing and the other for composition (1889). At this time, Stojowski's great fellow-countryman, Paderewski, assumed the educational care of his career and became his teacher in person. His orchestral compositions attracted wide attention in Paris, and he met with pronounced success as a virtuoso. With the opening of the new Institute of Musical Art [1906] under the direction of Mr. Frank Damrosch [1859-1937], Mr. Stojowski assumed the direction of the pianoforte department and under his care this department grew in a most flattering manner [1906-1912]. Mr. Stojowski, aside from his musical talent, is a remarkable linguist and speaks English with a fluency rarely associated with those of foreign birth. As he remarked to the interviewer, 'We Poles are given the credit for being natural linguists because we take the trouble to learn language thoroughly in our youth.' " [ETUDE, September 1911]. "As the lifelong friend and exponent of Paderewski, Mr. Stojowski has through innumerable conferences identified his ideas with those of the great master pianist. It is therefore unnecessary to do anything more than intimate the value of these lessons to those who realize the importance of interpretation in the pianoforte study." [ETUDE, November 1916].

Bibliographical Note: The golden age of THE ETUDE boasted exceptionally large trim sizes that accommodated images of the composer and/or the pianists designed around a very readable three-column text format. In the present edition, images were omitted to maximize textual content; which was reset in two-column format, and slightly edited to focus upon performance practice. Editorial insertions are made in square brackets. Staves were individually scanned and placed to avoid the characteristically "crowded" look of ETUDE music plates. Plates were also digitally enhanced to clean and sharpen the notation, and fingerings, pedal markings and written instructions were reset wherever it would improve legibility. THE ETUDE often counted pick-up measures as complete measures in numbering schemes. This was altered to match modern editions. Spelling and musical nomenclature were modernized. Obvious errors in the original text and plates were silently corrected.

Beethoven's "Contradance in C"
A Master Lesson by the Renowned Piano Virtuoso
MARK HAMBOURG
[December 1938]

The name *contradanse* is of English origin, being really only a corruption of the words *country dance*. The fashionable dance, in vogue in the eighteenth century France, was known as the Branle, but it was later superseded in favor by the contradanse anglaise, or English country dance. Already in 1699 a book: "Suite de Dances de Roi," compiled by one, [C.] Ballard [Paris, Bibliothèque nationale], was in existence in France, and it contained seventeen "contradanses anglaises." The contradanse is to be found also in French stage music of the time, having been introduced into the ballet of an opera by [Antoine] Dauvergne [1713-1797] called *Les Troqueurs* [1753].

The contradanse is always in either two-four or six-eight time; and it consists of similar phrases of eight measures each, which generally are repeated. The music is of a lively kind, and it was a popular form with eighteenth century composers.[1] Mozart left a large number of specimens, and Beethoven, himself, produced twelve contradanses for orchestra [WoO 14], of one of which [No. 1] the piano work we have here under consideration is a transcription.

The Music Begins
This *Contradanse* in C major, marked Allegro molto moderato, starts with an accompaniment in the bass, which must be given ponderously, as becomes a peasant dance. The grace notes in each measure, on the last eighth note, should be played incisively and sharply; and all the eighth notes of the bass must be very detached; but at the same time the rhythm should sound leisurely and somewhat bucolic. Up to the last beat of m. 2, the bass should be *mezzo piano*.

The sixteenth notes, with which the theme in the right hand is ushered in, on the last half of m. 2, must be played sharply, but with care to give the exact rhythmical value to each note. The music should be given weightily, but at the same time with humor; and the top notes of the right hand must be brought out, as they constitute the melody. The sixteenth notes on the last half-beat of m. 2, where the right hand makes its entry, must be played very deliberately, without any hurry. These sixteenth notes at the opening of the phrases occur several times throughout the first part of the piece; and whenever they appear they must be played in the same deliberate way.

In m. 3 there is a crescendo which culminates on the accented chord of C major in the treble, on the second beat of m. 4, and then decrescendos in m. 5. The accents should be very much marked on the chord C–E–G in the right hand on the second half of the first beat in m. 6, so that it acts as a complement to the accented note, C, in a similar position in m. 4. From mm. 6–9 there is a continuous crescendo, finishing with a *mezzo forte* in m. 10. The top notes, in the treble in m. 9, must be brought out with marked and detached rhythm, and with a little slowing down of tempo to signalize the definite end of the phrase, which comes on the first beat of m. 10, where there is an accent. A good pause must be made after the accented first beat of m. 10, and a little hesitancy be shown on the two sixteenth notes which make their entry in the right hand at the end of m. 10, so as to emphasize the return of the original theme

[1][To this point the text is a fairly literal rendering from *Grove's Dictionary of Music and Musicians*; the entry for "Contradanse," 1927, Vol. I, p. 708].

which occurs here. The tempo then resumes its normal course. Measures 11–17, inclusive, are a repetition of the opening measures, and must be played in the same way.

The Rustic Beau Now Bows
The phrase in the bass, beginning with two sixteenth notes, F and E, on the last half of the second beat in m. 18, must be introduced heavily, as though a somewhat clumsy countryman were dancing; and, although the tone should be *mezzo forte* at the commencement of this phrase in the left hand, still a progressive crescendo ought to be made up to the last half of m. 22. In m. 22, on the last two sixteenth notes, we find a new figure introduced, which really only constitutes a slightly more elaborate end of phrase. The running figure must be played brightly *forte*, and in a bustling manner, with a slight decrescendo at the end of m. 24. This decrescendo leads to two little accents on the first and second beats of m. 25, in the right hand, and there is another accent on the first beat of m. 26.

The chord at the beginning of m. 26 must be *mezzo piano* in tone, although weighty in touch. At the end of this m. 26 the same figure starts in the bass as in the end of m. 18, but this time, instead of a progressive crescendo being made, I make a progressive decrescendo with the short phrases very markedly rhythmical. When the decrescendo reaches m. 30, the tone has become *piano*, and I start the figure in the right hand on the last half of the second beat in this measure softly, but quickly make a crescendo and end the phrase *forte* in m. 33, with much gaiety in expression and giving the accents as marked.

Some Attractive Arpeggios
Having arrived at m. 34, we have a new development consisting of an upward arpeggio-like progression of notes. This progression should be played pompously, in stately fashion, and *fortissimo*. On the last beat of m. 36, I commence a diminuendo; but the incisive notes of the left hand, in m. 37, and the sixteenth note figures in the treble of this measure must still sound highly rhythmical; and to effect this they must be played without the pedal. The pedal should be retaken in the beginning of m. 38, and the trumpet-like chords in both hands, on the second half of the first beat, and on the first half of the second beat, ought to be played *pianissimo*, but very distinctly, the pedal being held from the first note of m. 38, as far as the last two sixteenth notes in that measure. The arpeggio-like development is repeated in mm. 39 and 40; and the two succeeding measures are the same as mm. 37 and 38, and must be played in a similar manner.

Coming to m. 41, I take the G in the left hand with the thumb of the right hand, instead of with the left hand—this to facilitate the execution. I do the same with the F♯ on the next beat of this measure, in the left hand part, taking it with the right hand thumb.

On arriving at m. 42, the grace notes in mm. 43–45, and both of those in m. 46, all must be very sharply played; and the accents, as marked, must be crisp. Also, all the staccato eighth notes in each of these measures must be emphasized. In m. 47 there is an accent on the first note in both hands, and then a progressive crescendo up to m. 49, where a sudden *pianissimo* ought to be made, which must last until the first half of the second beat in m. 50, on the eighth note top C. I take, again, the left hand notes on the first and second beats of m. 49, with the right hand as in m. 41. Measures 51–54 all should sound ponderous, with the grace notes of each measure accented, and with all the marked accents deeply interlined.

The scale, commencing in the right hand in m. 55, is accented on the first note, C; and then a diminuendo occurs gradually, up to the end of m. 56, when the tone becomes *mezzo forte* again and crescendos to double *forte* in m. 58. The rhythmical figures starting on the last two sixteenth notes of m. 58, in the bass, and lasting up to m. 63 (each hand echoing the other, and mounting in octaves) are played by me as follows: I take the two sixteenth notes, each time they appear [on either staff] with the second finger of the right hand; whilst the accented single dotted notes in the left hand, on the first beat of each of these measures, and the staccato eighth notes on the second beat, written in the right hand, I take with the thumb of the left hand. The whole of this episode should be brilliantly brought out, with a rising crescendo up to the note D in the treble in m. 62, on the second beat, where a fermata is marked. Here I make a considerable pause.

In Tenderer Mood

At the end of m. 62 we arrive at a new section, which takes the form of a charming, graceful melody. It should be performed rather slower, and with a more mellow expression, to distinguish it from the heavier atmosphere of the first part. Although most of this section is semi-staccato, it must not be played with such markedly detached action as the first section of the *Contradanse*.

In m. 67 the first [G] in the bass must have a little accent, and also the [D] in the treble; while in m. 68 there is a very pronounced accent on the chord on the second beat, in both hands. This chord should be held a trifle longer than its value, as if it formed the interrogation mark at the end of a question, the question being the phrase which occupies mm. 67–68 in the treble; the answer coming in m. 69, in *piano* tone, rather as an echo.

There is a little accent on the first note, D, in the bass of m. 69, and also one on the first octave on D, in the treble, on the second half of the first beat. [Four] notes, very much marcato, in mm. 70–71, should be played rather slower and with more vehemence. In m. 71 the tempo returns again to normal. Measures 75–77 are repetitions of mm. 67–69, only a little more ornamented, and must be played in the same way. The ensuing measures, commencing on the last half of the second beat of m. 78, and continuing to m. 102, find the left hand part equally prominent as the right hand; and the music should be played like two voices talking together, both the top notes and the bass being brought out with singing tones—mm. 79–82 being especially legato, as are also mm. 87–90. The bass notes in mm. 83 and 84 must be made especially prominent, with a crescendo in m. 84 culminating in an accent on the top E, quarter note, on the second beat of this measure; whilst both of these measures should be a little ritenuto.

All the bass notes in m. 85 must be brought out, and a further accent should be given on the first note, high G, in the left hand in m. 86. Measures 87–94 are similar to mm. 79–86. Measure 95 is a repetition, in *pianissimo*, of m. 93. Measure 97 should be *mezzo piano*, with a little crescendo, which sinks to *piano* again in m. 98.

Though the left hand staccato notes in m. 99 are *pianissimo*, yet they, too, lead up to a little crescendo at the end of the measure, which, however, drops immediately again on the first note of m. 100. A little crescendo appears again at the end of m. 100, and leads to an accent on the first and third eighth notes of m. 101, all of this being in the left hand.

All Joys Have an End

In m. 102 a little ritenuto must be made, to prepare for the return of the original subject, which is ushered in at m. 103. All the staccato notes, which form the passage in the left hand, especially from m. 96 to the end of these passages in m. 102, must be played exactly and crisply, with a coy kind of humor, the accents being strictly observed and marked. At m. 102, just after the last eighth note in the bass, there should be a breath pause, the solo left hand being lifted off the keys before attacking the bass C on the first beat of m. 103, where the *tempo primo* reappears. This *tempo primo* ought to be played with the same accents, and in the same way, as the first seventeen measures of the piece; only the level of tone should now be a little less loud, and a little less pointed.

From the last half of the second beat in m. 120, where there are sixteenth notes in both hands, there should be a brilliant *fortissimo*, which proceeds onwards through mm. 121–123, to terminate in a sforzando on the G octave on the first beat of m. 124. In mm. 125 and 126, I make a crescendo during the sixteenth note figures in the treble, as I have marked in the piece, so as to get the true Beethovenesque effect of the sudden *mezzo piano* at the beginning of m. 127. Measure 129 is *pianissimo*, like an answer or an echo to m. 127. Measures 131 and 132 ought to be played with singing tone, and plaintively, with a very marked ritenuto, as though the dancers were viewing the speedy drawing to a close of the dance, with sentimental regret; whilst the last two chords of the work, on the second beat of m. 133, and on the first beat of the final measure, must, by contrast, be very loud and abrupt, emphasizing the fact that the dance is definitely at an end.

The fun is over.

The whole of the piece must be played with a sparing use of the right pedal.

Contradance [No. 1]

L. van BEETHOVEN

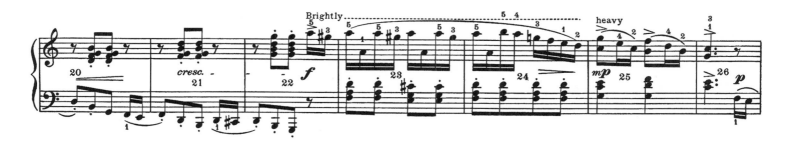

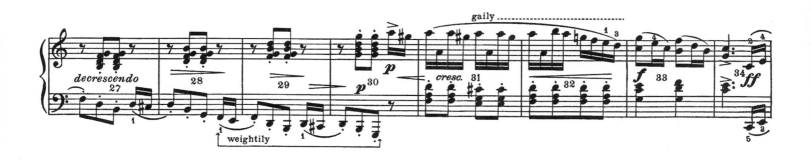

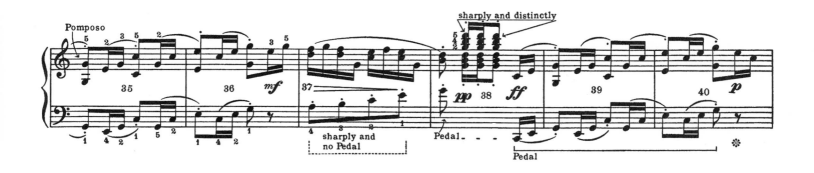

A Master Lesson Upon Beethoven's Sonata Pathétique

Prepared Expressly for THE ETUDE by the Eminent Piano Virtuoso

WILHELM BACHAUS
[October 1926]

The Sonatas of Ludwig van Beethoven, standing as classical pillars in the great art of music, continually afford opportunities for study, investigation and admiration.

Beethoven's compositions when they first appeared were regarded as extremely modernistic, almost as many in this day might look upon the compositions of Stravinsky, Bartók or Scriabine. For instance, Ignaz Moscheles [1794-1870] describes his first acquaintance with the *Sonata Pathétique*.

> "About this time I heard from some fellow-students that there was a composer recently come to the fore in Vienna who wrote the most curious stuff in the world—a baroque type of music, contrary to all rules, which no one could play and no one could understand; the composer's name was Beethoven. To satisfy my curiosity as to this eccentric genius, I betook myself to the lending library and procured a copy of Beethoven's *Sonata Pathétique*. I had not enough money to buy the work, but I secretly copied it out. I found the novel style so attractive, and my admiration was so enthusiastic, that I so far forgot myself as to mention my new discovery to my teacher. He thereupon reminded me of his precepts, and warned me not to play or study eccentric productions until my style was formed on more reliable examples. I disregarded this advice and acquired Beethoven's works one by one as they appeared, finding in them such consolation and delight as no other composer was able to give me."

The brilliant French critic and novelist, Romain Rolland [1866-1944] (author of *Jean Christophe*), finds it difficult to see why Beethoven called this sonata the *Sonata Pathétique*, except for the "sad and dramatic introduction theme." The same author, however, draws our attention to the fact that in 1799, when the sonata was produced, Beethoven was just becoming conscious of the great tragedy of his life—his approaching deafness.

In this sonata, Beethoven saw fit to omit the conventional minuet (as he did also in Opus 10, No. 1). The work is distinctly different in type from Beethoven's later work. One writer points out that it is more the prelude to an oncoming tragedy than the tragedy itself. Beethoven's employment of diminished-seventh chords in the introduction is in keeping with his apparent practice of using these chords to express sadness and pain.

Before making a detailed analysis of the *Sonata Pathétique*, I would like to make a few remarks concerning the interpretation of the works of Beethoven, in general. You will discover in the compositions of Beethoven, even in his earliest works, occasional temperamental outbursts, such as are not to be found in the music of any composer prior to his time. This, in combination with many stories current about Beethoven's proverbial bad temper—which according to reports was supposed to have manifested itself in such incidents as throwing a chair or a plate or a cup at his servants, and other displays of uncontrollable anger—leads some mistaken students to the belief that they will catch the right spirit in which to interpret the masterpieces of the great romantic composer by playing certain passages with violent shakings of the head, throwing the arms about or otherwise punishing the piano. The result of such a performance is comparable with that of a snarling, growling lapdog rather than a true interpretation of the real power and majesty of the Titan Beethoven.

It should be understood that Beethoven did not make his art the playground for any exhibitions of his bad humors. We cannot in this age divine what may have gone on in Beethoven's mind and soul in meeting the obstacles, provocations and irritations brought to him by his servants and acquaintances, to say nothing of his sad fate. Therefore, it is not fair for us to criticize the great master. We have only to admire the magnificent manner in which he emerged spiritually and with greater soul power from every affliction which befell him. It is true that some storm of passion or some torrent of rage may have been the source of some of his inspirations. These were not manifested in his works, because of his interminable process of laboring to refine and mould his ideas into the great works of art which will forever remain in their final perfected form, among the treasured possessions of cultured mankind.

Hurried Writing

Beethoven did not throw his compositions upon paper in a rage or in a hurry. On the other hand, he laboriously kept note books in which he jotted down his ideas. He kept remolding and improving the themes and their development painstakingly ridding them of all ignoble and superficial ingredients, so that in the end they become the very quintessence, the most intense and exalted expression of the original inspiration. In this you will find no bad humor, but rather a majestic aloofness, a firm and grim determination to conquer fate, a revelation of gigantic strength of purpose. The interpreter who tries to embody this in his work will ascend to somewhere near the lofty plane where Beethoven's works rightly belong.

In the words of my famous teacher, Eugène d'Albert [1864-1932], in his notes to the Beethoven G Major Concerto, "One must seek to interpret master works himself with the great spirituality of the composer, submerging one's own, probably far lesser, individuality."

It should be superfluous to mention that a perfect mastery of the technical side of any musical composition is the fundamental condition leading to its best interpretation.

Outdoing the Player-Piano

There seems to be a popular idea that since the player-pianos of the higher type can reproduce the notes of a composition with remarkable accuracy as to notes, time, rhythm, and all technical details, the performer in public should go to extremes in doing "more than that." That is, he should exercise all kinds of liberties and distort his interpretations into what is popularly conceived as "emotional playing." In such playing, allowance is made even for "wrong notes" as manifestations of the human element.

Of course, this is a fatal error, as only the perfect combination of all factors such as tone, technic, heart and intellect can be called art as distinguished from dilettantism. Even though the design of a building may be perfection in itself, if in the execution of that design there should be a mistake in the construction or an insufficient support anywhere, the building is likely to collapse. In similar manner any wrong note in the interpretation of a piece, any passage that is not perfectly shaped will be a blemish upon the work performed. Therefore we cannot consider the interpretation of a work apart from the technical mastery. The two form an indivisible whole. Beethoven's own very strong views upon this are indicated in his letters to Czerny, who was teaching Beethoven's nephew, in which he dwelt upon the importance of scale study.

The Printed Plan

It is this which adds infinite charm to the art of musical performance. The printed music is nothing more than the composer's design. It resembles, in distant manner, the architect's plans, except that the architect must build in stone, steel, brick or marble, while the musical artist must erect with each performance a fairy structure of tones which dissolve into the listener's memories the moment they are played. The only way in which they may be preserved is by some of the playing devices, such as the Duo-Art, the Welte-Mignon, or the Ampico. No artist plays a composition precisely alike each time. Rarely do the interpretations of two artists more than approximate in their executions of the composer's notes his designs of the same composition. Therefore, the interest in musical interpretation is so varied that it is undying. Yet this does not mean that any great interpreters ever seek to exaggerate their interpretations. On the other hand, they are continually seeking, painstakingly and conscientiously, to come as near as possible to the composer's meaning. Notwithstanding this, the variations in the human mind and the human soul, to say nothing of the nervous and muscular systems, are so great that every interpretation is different.

The Sonata's Character

The character of *Sonata Pathétique* is determined by the severe and sombre nature of the introduction, which, though only ten measures long, is intensely dramatic. It bears the tempo mark, *Grave*, and the metronomic marking, ♪ = 69. This is given in some editions as ♪ = 66. Beethoven was for years an intimate friend of [Johannes] Maelzel [1772-1838], the inventor of the metronome. He labored to help Maelzel introduce his invention, but after the two friends had quarreled, Beethoven said, "Don't let us have any metronome. He that hath true feeling will not require it, and for him who has none, it will not be of any use."

The movement commences with stern *forte* chords, all seven notes of which should be struck at once. Any suggestion of raggedness here would destroy the entire impression of the movement. Kindly watch the pedal marks in this edition very closely. The pedal marks have been indicated very carefully. For the beginner, it is unnecessary to use the pedal more than marked. The *Sonata* permits of great variation in pedaling; but, as I have said, the notes themselves are no more than the design of the structure, and it would be literally impossible to insert all of the pedalings which an artist would instinctively use. Nor would this be desirable in the edition, because they would demand so much detailed and skilled practice that the student might misinterpret directions given without personal explanations and opportunities for experiment under the teacher. In general, however, the pedal should always be depressed after striking the chord, not with it. This is one of the first rules of pedaling. Another is that the release of the pedal at a definite moment is just as important as its introduction. The pedal is a tone blender; its employment is infinite in results and should be a subject for lifelong experiment of the serious artist.

Use of Pedal

The pedal should be released after the first chord, precisely as indicated, before the next phrase which begins *piano* and ascends to an effective crescendo followed by a decrescendo. The second measure has the same expressional complexion as the first. Careful attention should be given in the first three important measures, to Beethoven's quite evident purpose

to have the dynamic force develop with increasing intensity, reaching the crest of the wave upon the first chord of m. 4, when the composition seems to become broader and broader, attaining a still further climax in the middle of the measure on the solitary A♭ in the right hand.

In m. 3, the student should take particular care to preserve the tempo accurately, and not be deceived into exaggerating the thirty-second rest. Comparatively few students play this measure quite correctly as there is an aural deception.

The dot over the fourth chord (F minor triad), in the fourth measure, does not mean staccato. The chord should be held just long enough to take the pedal, then both right and left hands should be released. In the nine-note group, terminating the run in m. 4, the first four notes should be played in strict time as 128th notes followed by the group of five at a proportionately accelerated speed. The run should not be hurried.

Beethoven's Diminished-Sevenths

In m. 5 the composition changes temporarily to major, seeming to lose for the time being its forbidding character, for the first three-fourths of the measure, but this is harshly contradicted by the forceful diminished-seventh chords immediately following. Again, let me urge, do not punish the keyboard with violence here. The chords should be sombre and majestic without any suggestion of anger.

The beginning of the Allegro di molto seems to be for most students the signal for a great rush, a furious onslaught. That, however, is a wrong idea. There should be something mysterious about it; at the same time, it must be absolutely clean and crisp in touch, an even *piano*, with perfect rhythm (neither accelerando nor crescendo in m. 14). Even the first chord in m. 15 is still *piano*. Always remember Hans von Bülow's maxim, "Crescendo means *piano*, diminuendo means *forte*."

This, doubtless, came from von Bülow's experience in teaching pupils to whom the sign crescendo meant loud, instead of growing from soft to loud, and vice versa with decrescendo. It is advisable to take the left pedal for measures 11 and 12. The *sf* in m. 13, which, by the way, must not be exaggerated, should, however, have a little support by a small accent in the left hand. Watch the decrescendo in m. 18, so that mm. 19–20 will be a real *piano* again.

At the entry of the second theme (in m. 51) do not let the left hand go over the right and the right in turn jump over the left, but rather pass the left hand *under* the right, which you can do very comfortably during m. 50, and the right will be easily within reach of the B♭ in m. 51. The tempo slows down just a trifle during mm. 49 and 50. The section from mm. 51–88 contains the most difficult passage in the whole movement, although it may not look it. I am referring to the series of mordents. They should be played, as marked in m. 57, all the way through and should never be allowed to degenerate into triplets, which would make the whole passage appear insipid and trivial. This is very difficult and requires a lot of patient practice. I find that the safest fingering is 2–3–2, each time, with the first on the following notes, with the exception of

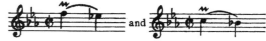

as in those cases it is almost impossible to bring the first on the black key with perfect elegance, and therefore the fingering must be 3–4–3, with the second finger on the following quarter note. The little phrase

must at all times be staccato all four notes, as also the three notes:

in mm. 52, 60, and others. There seems to be a temptation for some pupils to slur the F with the G♭ in the following measure, which must be absolutely avoided.

There should also be no crescendo in those three notes, as it would merely weaken the significance of the expressive melodious *sf* in mm. 53, 54 and other similar ones. The appoggiatura B♭ in m. 53 (and similar measures) comes *on* the beat, not before. The whole passage should be played espressivo and cantabile, not hurried; M.M. ♩=138. The second part of the theme (mm. 56–59) should be given with more tone and significance in the repetition of m. 76, and again even more so in m. 80, from which point the theme should broaden and become more tranquil in tempo (not so much, however, as to call it ritardando) and diminish in tone to a soft *pianissimo* in m. 88. Now the next four measures should be played *piano*, from m. 93 (crescendo means *piano*, a very gradual crescendo, as it is not to reach a *forte* until m. 99). The phrasing,

which looks rather forbidding at first, is to be understood more in a spiritual sense and may have been inspired by the thought of the passage played on the violin, where the phrasing would be actually carried out as indicated and would result in that perfectly natural emphasis of the first note of each group, without any thought of a real accent. This is exactly what Beethoven seems to want here; the first note of each group to be struck with decision and not to be held, in contrast with the four measures preceding, which still have a more tranquil character, indicated by the whole and half notes which should be carefully given their full value.

In m. 113, there is a sudden *piano* on the second quarter. The right hand passage here should be practiced to great perfection and evenness, and should appear like a ball rolling down the hillside, of its own weight. The bass notes, C, A♭, and B♭, should be slightly accentuated in mm. 114 and 116 and stronger in mm. 118 and 120.

It will be a useful lesson for my readers to put in the pedal marks themselves in the passage from mm. 223–286, as it corresponds with the passage in the first part of the Allegro, which I have marked carefully [mm. 51–116].

In m. 297, we find the resumption of the *Grave*. In 297–300, the passage should be cumulative in intensity, and in m. 299 it might even be permissible to become broader in tempo. However, there should be no further ritenuto in m. 300. The concluding six descending chords in mm. 299–300 should be played with beautiful legato and decrescendo.

The mm. 301–304 should be again *piano*, without accelerando or crescendo, which latter is reserved for mm. 305–307 and works out as follows:

$$p \quad mf \mid f \;\lt\; \mid ff$$
$$305 \qquad 306 \qquad 307$$

It is obvious that it would spoil the meaning and the effect of this quick crescendo, if you were to start it before m. 305.

A Poetical Analysis

In order to recapitulate, I would like to add a few words suggesting a poetical analysis of this movement, as it has forced itself on my mind. The opening theme (m. 1) divides in two sections, namely the *forte* chord and the pleading motive.

Let me suggest the name "opposition" for the *forte* chord, and it will then appear that the hero finds opposition in his way right at the start, and he tries to conquer it by pleading. This repeats three times, the pleading the third time being the most intense by virtue of dynamics, tonal height and repetition. We will notice the number three playing quite an important part as we go on. In mm. 5–7, we find the pleading theme again, three times with increasing intensity interrupted by opposing forces (to the rhythm ♪♪ thrice repeated). This is the last time the opposition speaks in *fortissimo* and it seems to retire exhausted for the time being. The hero sets to work right away (Allegro di molto e con brio) with the theme of attack (mm. 11–15) which means unceasing toil, and already in mm. 38 and 42, we seem to hear parts of some Chinese wall falling down, and more so in mm. 45–48. This is where the hero relaxes in his work, given to more tender reflections. The phrase

appears three times up to m. 71 and then is followed by the phrase

in three repetitions, intensified each time by the change in key. Still the rest can be only temporary and work begins again in m. 89, at first *piano* and carefully, but working to a climax in mm. 99–100. A new start is made and a higher climax reached in 111–112. Having achieved that much, the hero has a few moments of real joy and the mm. 113–120, have certainly some likeness to a little boy rolling himself down a hill on a fine summer's day. However, in m. 121, he picks himself up in a second, for some new heroic effort, of which the chord in m. 134 is the final blow, *fortissimo*. (The repetition seems to be indicated more by adherence to the old-fashioned form than by inner necessity and is better ignored.) Now, *Tempo I, Grave*. Opposition is still there, threatening three times, and three times the pleading theme is heard, but this time not with greatest intensity the third time, but retiring into *pianissimo*, as if the hero had recognized that only effort would help, and pleading be of no avail. And new efforts are made (Allegro molto). Some haunting fears and doubts (mm. 169–172 and 177–180) have to be conquered by the phrase in m. 183 repeated three times. A run of eight measures leads to the recapitulation of the principal subject of the *Allegro*, which we have called "the theme of attack." It loses some of its sternness by the modulation into D♭ from mm. 210–213, which passage is repeated three times with growing intensity. This leads once more into the passage of tender thoughts (the mordente episode) and through renewed activities with the two climaxes to the feeling of exhilaration from m. 279. The theme of attack again leads to a grand climax in 296. Now follow four measures of the greatest significance. Opposition apparently being entirely overcome, mm. 297–299, each begins with absolute void. All the same, the pleading theme appears three times with increasing intensity, in fact the third time with greater intensity than ever before, almost an outcry, as if the loneliness of the victor was even harder to bear than opposition and struggle. A touching illustration of the solitude of greatness. Still, to quote Schiller, the strong man is mightiest by himself, and the movement closes with an overpowering assertion of strength.

Although the *Sonata Pathétique* bears the early opus number 13, and is a work of Beethoven's first period, written before the age of thirty, the intensity of its appeal is so strong that we can only put it in a line with his greatest master works.

Concentrate all the energy psychic and physical, you have on the final four chords, which should be struck with vehemence and strictly together—striking the chords from a distance above the keyboard, with a combined movement of lower arm and wrist, which will bring the *Sonata* to a majestic and significant close.

Dedicated to Prince von Lichnowsky

SONATA PATHÉTIQUE

L. van Beethoven, Op. **13**

a) Of these 9 notes, four may be regarded as strict 128ths and the remainder as a group of five.

The "Ballade, Op. 10, No. 1" of Brahms

A Master Lesson by the Renowned Piano Virtuoso
MARK HAMBOURG

[November 1938]

The old Scottish Ballad "Edward" is blood-curdling and dramatic to a degree; and the well known vocal setting of it, by Johann [Carl Gottfried] Loewe [1796-1869], is in the form of a duologue between a mother and son; the mother questioning the son about the blood she sees upon him. He at first answers that he has killed his hawk; then that he has killed his horse; and at last confesses that it is his father whom he has killed. The mother continues to ply him with questions as to what penance he will do, and what will become of his family and lands if he flees the country, as he says he must. Finally she asks what will become of herself, if he leaves her. Here, in a great climax of horror, he turns upon her with curses, saying that it was she who persuaded him to murder the father.

And Now We Interpret

The work must be played in a narrative manner throughout. The first eight measures, up to the fourth beat of m. 8, must be performed with a hollow sound, as if someone were talking in a toneless voice; in fact, almost in a whisper. This effect can be produced by using very little pedal, laying no stress on the melody, and only now and then emphasizing slightly the notes so marked. By this manner of playing, an ominous, apprehensive feeling is imparted to the music.

There is a slight rise in tone on the second beat of m. 1, and a decrescendo towards the end of the measure; whilst the two eighth-note chords, on the second beat in both hands, must be played semi-legato, so as to differentiate them from the rest of the music, which is consistently legato throughout the first twenty-six measures, except where these two chords appear on the second beat of any measure; thus, in D minor, as in mm. 1, 4, 14, and 17, and in G minor, as in mm. 5 and 18, when they must be always semi-legato.

In m. 2 there is a slight emphasis on the quarter-note chord on the first beat in both hands, and again on the last quarter in the measure; also on the first, second and third beats of m. 3, with this difference; that the notes E and A, on the second and third beats of m. 3, must sound like an echo of the notes E on the last beat of m. 2 and A on the first beat of m. 3.

On reaching m. 5, the last quarter-note G in the treble of this measure must sink down to the dotted half note on C♯ in the following measure, with a kind of groan; and the half-note B♭ in the bass, on the second beat of m. 6, should be emphasized. Again the progression from the C♯ octave in the right hand (bass clef), on the last beat of m. 6, to the dotted half-note octave D on the first beat of m. 7, must sound like an echo of the groan in the preceding measure—almost a deep sigh.

At the end of m. 7, the G♯ (bass clef), on the fourth beat of the right hand, proceeds in a similar manner to the dotted half-note A in the next measure, and must be played in the same sighing manner, only more slowly and more *pianissimo*, whilst an accent must be made on the second beat [F] in m. 7, on the bass clef, just as on the second beat in m. 6.

The Significance Increases

From the last beat of m. 8, where it is marked Poco piu moto, to the third beat of m. 13, more body must be introduced into the music, and the tempo should be slightly quickened. The melody in the treble should be brought out; and, though marked *mezzo piano*, it must be played with a fuller tone than the music of the first eight measures.

In m. 10, although it is imperative that every note be kept absolutely legato, the hands must be lifted from the keys, after the dotted quarter note on the third beat (without, however, taking off the pedal), before playing the succeeding eighth-note chord; thus making what I call a "breath" pause, which serves to give elasticity to the phrasing of the melody. Then continuing to the first beat of m. 11, a tiny pause should be made after this beat, to introduce a repetition of the theme which now recurs, but in a different tonality. This development must be played a little slower, and the tempo should further decrease, until a fermata is reached on the third beat of m. 13, where a long pause must be made. The middle notes of the treble chords in m. 12, namely, E♭ and D, must be brought out; also the D, C♯, and E♮ in the same position in the chords of the next measure; as these notes constitute an inner melody. Also a small accent must be given to the B♭ on the first beat of the treble in m. 13.

From the last beat of m. 13, to m. 21, is a reiteration of the first eight measures of the piece, which must be played in the same manner.

On the fourth beat of m. 21 we reach Poco piu moto, again, and to this section of five measures (22–26) must be given an intimate and reflective atmosphere, the music being very legato and the top notes of the melody being brought out, without, however, smothering the accompaniment. The breath pause, as described in m. 10, should be made after the third beat of m. 23. The volume of tone, though *piano*, must be full and round; and, from the last beat of m. 21 onward through mm. 22–23, the playing should be more tuneful and colorful than in the succeeding measures (24–25) where the tone must sink to *pianissimo*.

A Call to Combat

The hands must be lifted from the keys, between the first and second beats of m. 24, so as to mark the change to the softer tone which follows. Upon reaching m. 26 there is a small crescendo during the progression of the two chords on the first and second beats of this measure, leading to the fermata on the third beat; and also a little ritardando, the endeavor being to try to produce the effect of a question.

We come now, at the fourth beat of m. 26, to a new development of the *Ballade*, which is marked Allegro ma non troppo (lively, but not too much so). Here we have a martial theme in the left hand part, which ought to produce a tone as though being played by a brass instrument; soft and insistent in the beginning, and supported by the pedal, but without any staccato attack. This martial subject continues, with ever increasing tone, up to the third beat of m. 43. The accompaniment of triplet chords, dealt with by the right hand, should strive to imitate a roll of drums, muffled to start with, but gradually growing, in a crescendo, until it reaches its apex in m. 37, with a great *fortissimo*. This *fortissimo* is continued throughout mm. 38–43 inclusive; and the tempo should be slower in the last four of these measures. On the last beat of m. 43 the music returns to the second subject of the piece, which has been already described in m. 9, in a different tonality, at Poco piu moto; only now it is amplified in style, and the chords and octaves, of which it is composed, are played heavily and loudly. The triplet eighth notes in the bass, on the last beat of m. 43, must be stressed.

Coming to m. 45, the hands must be taken off the keys before taking the final eighth-note chord, so as to usher in the succeeding phrase, as is done in *piano* tone in m. 10; but in m. 45 the tone remains consistently *forte*. An accent must be made on the last chord in m. 45, and also one on the first chord in m. 46; for these accents give point to the phrasing. Again, in m. 48, the hands are lifted before playing the C minor chords; whilst these chords and the one on the first beat of m. 49 are accented. In mm. 50 and 51, a similar progression of chords occurs, where the accents should be made on the last chord of m. 50, and on the first chord of m. 51, and the hands lifted before taking the last chord in m. 50, as in mm. 45 and 48. This lifting of the hands at the finish of a phrase, without removing the pedal, helps to give both significance to the phrase and grace to the execution. From the fourth beat of m. 48 to the middle of m. 54, the single notes in the left hand, which constitute the subject, should be made prominent, and should sound through the rest of the music, in juxtaposition to the melodic theme, which is played in the treble.

In m. 52 I take the bass C (which is written in the music for the left hand) with the right hand, as it is easier thus.

A Melancholy Denouement

The volume of sound diminishes from m. 53 onwards, until it reaches *pianissimo* on the dotted half-note chord on the second beat of m. 57, in the bass; but, though *pianissimo*, this chord must be played with emphasis. When this insistent chord is repeated in m. 58, on the second beat, I find it better to take it with the right hand, so as to allow the descending phrase—A and G in eighth notes in m. 58, and F and E in m. 59—to lie easily under the fingers of the left hand.

On the fourth beat of m. 59 we return to the original subject of the work, but embellished by triplets in the left hand. These triplets must be played with absolute exactitude as to their rhythmic value, and staccato. The interpretation here must be the same as in the beginning of the *Ballade*, only more dramatically expressed, in order to stress the atmosphere of tragedy which culminates on the suspended chord on the last beat of m. 69. The progression from the chord on the last beat of m. 64, in the treble, proceeding to the following one on the first beat of m. 65, must sound like a question, the answer coming from the similar chord progression from the last beat of m. 65 to the first beat of m. 66.

The ultimate five measures of the *Ballade* bring it to a close in a mood of deepest melancholy.

Classes with Hans von Bülow
by Harriette Brower
[combined from *Piano Mastery Vol. 1 1917* and *THE ETUDE September 1912*]

Those who heard Hans von Bülow in recital during his American tour, in 1876, listened to piano playing that was at once learned and convincing. He was a deep thinker and analyzer; as he played one saw, as though reflected in a mirror, each note, phrase and dynamic mark of expression to be found in the work. After hearing von Bülow the impulse was to hasten to the instrument and reproduce what had just seemed so clear and logical, so simple and attainable. It did not seem to be such a difficult thing to play the piano—like that! It was as though he had said: "Any of you can do what I am doing, if you will give the same amount of time and study to it that I have done. Listen and I will teach you!"

Toward the end of a season during the eighties, it was announced that von Bülow would come to Berlin and teach an artist class in the Klindworth Conservatory. This was an unusual opportunity to obtain lessons from so famous a musician and pedagogue, and about twenty pianists were enrolled for the class.

It was a bright May morning when the Director entered the music-room with his guest, and presented him to the class. They saw in him a man rather below medium height, with large intellectual head, beneath whose high, wide forehead shone piercing dark eyes, hidden behind glasses.

He bowed to the class, saying he was pleased to see so many industrious students. His movements, as he looked around the room, were quick and alert; he seemed to see everything at once, and the students saw that nothing could escape that active mentality.

The class met four days in each week, and the lessons continued from nine in the morning until well on toward one o'clock. It was announced that only the works of Brahms, Raff, Mendelssohn and Liszt would be taught and played, so nothing else need be brought to the class; indeed Brahms was to have the place of honor.

While many interesting compositions were discussed and played, perhaps the most helpful thing about these hours spent with the great pedagogue was the running fire of comment and suggestion regarding technic, interpretation, and music and musicians in general. Von Bülow spoke in rapid, nervous fashion, with a mixture of German and English, often repeating in the latter tongue what he had said in the former, out of consideration for the Americans and English present.

In teaching, von Bülow required the same qualities which were so patent in his playing. Clearness of touch, exactness in phrasing and fingering were the first requirements; the delivery of the composer's idea must be just as he had indicated it—no liberties with the text were ever permitted. He was so honest, so upright in his attitude toward the makers of good music, that it was a sin in his eyes to alter anything in the score, though he believed in adding any marks of phrasing or expression which would elucidate the intentions of the composer. Everything he said or did showed his intellectual grasp of the subject; and he looked for some of the same sort of intelligence on the part of the student.

One day, a young artist was playing a *Ballade* of Brahms, the one founded on the sinister poem on Edward. The opening of this first *Ballade* is sad, sinister and mysterious, like the old Scotch story. The master insisted on great smoothness in playing it—the chords to sound like muffled but throbbing heartbeats. A strong climax is worked up on the second page, which dies away on the third to a *pianissimo* of utter despair. From the middle of this page on to the end, the descending chords and octaves were likened to ghostly footsteps, while the broken triplets in the left hand accompaniment seem to indicate drops of blood. Toward the end of the second page the notes descend far down in the bass. The player was hastening to turn the leaf. "Stop!" cried von Bülow, from the other end of the room. "We have been in the deepest dungeon, and on the other side of that page comes a ray of sunshine; you must make a pause there, between the dark and the light, it is very effective."

BALLADE

After the Scottish Ballad "Edward"
in Herder's "Stimmen der Völker."

JOHANNES BRAHMS, Op. 10, No. 1

The Hungarian Dance, No. 6
by Johannes Brahms

* * * *

A Master Lesson

By

MAURICE DUMESNIL

[October 1939]

Of course everyone is familiar with this Hungarian Dance. It is one of Brahms' most popular compositions and certainly a favorite among the two sets written by the master in 1869, originally for piano, four hands. Many instrumental combinations have been published, including orchestra and band, and one hears it frequently over the air. Hence the question arises at first thought: was it advisable to devote a lesson to an arrangement, and more, to a simplified version?

The answer is most decidedly in the affirmative. Here is a very brilliant recital piece, full of color, rhythm and that fascinating *Magyar Stimmung* (tuning of the scale); certainly an excellent number for closing a group, or a program. In a more concise form, it contains some of the elements typical of the Liszt "Rhapsodies." The original two hand version is derived from the four hand score first conceived, however, and it is practically unplayable in the correct tempo, because it is overloaded with notes and the intervals are most awkward. Of the many pianists whom we have heard play it, none actually respected the text. One of these occasions was when François Planté [1839-1934], dean of the French pianists who died a few years ago close to his ninety-sixth birthday, performed it at one of his last Paris appearances. This was one of his favorite encore pieces, and his interpretation of it was supremely distinctive, elegant and aristocratic. He was, in his heyday, a rival of Liszt and Anton Rubinstein, and it was the latter who once said: "This Planté, he can play my *Valse Caprice* better than I do!" Indeed, while Rubinstein played the middle section *fortissimo*, and often fell out, Planté reached for those high notes gracefully and *pianissimo*, treating them like gems. He probably played this dance better than the natives!

Later, I heard Emanuel Moór [1863-1931] go through it in his own improvised fashion, one day when his rambling thoughts led him on the subject of the Hungarian folklore. Moór was born near Budapest, and throughout his life he remained unfalteringly attached to the melodies of his native land, despite the fact that he became a British citizen and ultimately lived in Switzerland. The inventor of the double-keyboard piano which bears his name admired greatly the Brahms "Hungarian Dances" but he contended that they were generally played without the proper tradition and were often disfigured into "salon music," thus losing their nobility and their atmosphere of languorous violins and frenzied dancers.

A Unique Contribution

The "Hungarian Dances" occupy a special place in the production of Brahms. He always insisted that they were mere adaptations of genuine popular tunes. Nevertheless, they bear in their working-out the unmistakable stamp of the master and show us that, next to his symphonies, quartets, trios and sonatas, he could be equally successful when handling the smaller and lighter forms. In fact the native music of Hungary exercised upon him an actual influence, and it is not uncommon to hear some of it in his chamber music productions, one striking example being the finale of the "Piano Quartet in G minor."

If we consider the date of Brahms' birth, 1833, we find that these "Dances" belong to the already mature period of his career, despite their fresh, youthful and alert spirit.

The *Dance No. 6* is simple and almost classical in structure. With the exception of a few measures (51–54 go into F major), it remains steadily in the key of D, oscillating between major and minor. The two "ideas" of the first part [m. 1 and m. 22] branch likewise into [similar closing phrases, m. 13 and 34] differently treated in each instance. The Andante constitutes the trio, with its accustomed da capo and coda.

The opening measure must be played in such a way as to set the scenery and create the atmosphere. Be careful not to attack before being thoroughly prepared. Much of the effect of any performance depends upon this initial impression. Consequently, it is recommended, after sitting down, to take time, get the fingers ready, set the wrists, and concentrate the mind upon the quality of tone to be extracted from the keyboard. *Mental attitude* must always precede *technical realization*.

The first chord is played loud and wrenched off the keys; and, in spite of the dot, one must push down powerfully and into the full depth, in order to avoid dryness. Do not be afraid to lift the right hand at least seven or eight inches high, so the second beat can take its proper aspect. We can compare this motion to that of a rubber ball striking the ground, rebounding, and falling down to stay put.

Measure 2 is played *a capriccio*, with fantasy, as if hesitating. The tempo has suddenly slowed down. The triplet in sixteenth notes can be interpreted thus:

in order to avoid a sluggish feeling. The dotted notes with legato sign indicate a portamento (non-staccato) which continues in the next measures, up to the vivo. The tempo should be slightly picked up in mm. 3–5, and also 7–9. Measure 6 is played like m. 2. At m. 5 lift the hand again as at the opening, but this time with charm and elegance; the wrist should be held flexible and the grace notes delivered fast. Measures 10–12 are a repetition of 2–4; still, the ritardando must be more pronounced and the volume of tone tapered off. Throughout this first portion it is advisable to bring out the upper notes in the right hand, slightly more than the lower ones; however difficult this may appear, it can easily be done by a slight stiffening of the fingers concerned. It is good practice to exaggerate at first and to play the upper notes *forte* and the lower notes *piano*; thereafter the volume can be adjusted to the suitable proportion. Let us think of this passage as being played by two clarinets, the first one more clearly heard than the second. Orchestral performances constantly call, on the part of the conductor, for delicate and even infinitesimal tonal adjustments of this kind, and pianists can derive much profit from developing their imagination along similar lines.

At the vivo (m. 13) there comes a complete change, and it occurs very abruptly, as a surprise. One must pass from lingering freedom to sharp rhythm and revert brusquely to the decision of the opening. No more rubato.

Contrasts are most effective when their constitutive elements work together in well balanced proportion. In the present case:

1. Tempo (here the sostenuto becomes vivo).
2. Shading (the *piano* turns to a *forte*).
3. Expression (the improvisation-like delivery becomes a fiery, dynamic rhythm).

At m. 19, it is a tradition to let down the tempo slightly, after striking the B, and to carry this through to m. 21, where the figure in sixteenth notes must be played once more with snap and crispness.

"Spirit" and "Basses"

The second "idea" extends over mm. 22–33. Here is where one can use plenty of dash and fire! Special attention is to be given to the left hand; two different kinds of attack are used: the notes on the beats must be strongly marked, while those off beat are played more lightly and superficially. It was Charles-Marie Widor [1844-1937] who once said: "The pianists do not play enough basses," in which he was right, since the basses are the foundation of the harmonic edifice and to neglect them means the collapse of the whole structure.

At m. 34, the contrast is purely of dynamics. Non-legato touch is used in the left hand while the right hand brings out the upper notes of the chords like a percussion effect, or as a piccolo would come through, somewhat shrilly, in an orchestral performance.

The run at m. 39 must convey the impression of a skyrocket soaring upward; and, after the top note, the hand and the forearm go up frankly, then fall back on the B where once more the tempo is let down slightly through the next measure.

The Andante brings a new element; it is dramatic and somewhat pompous, but the phrase retains a great character of dignity and stateliness, which should prompt us as to the keynote of the interpretation. Here the tone must be rich and full. The sonorous octaves in the bass are separated, but attacked with much weight from the forearm.

Measure 46 is played *martellato* (hammered, detached) in both hands. Be exceedingly careful to keep strict time, and be sure not to hurry. Every sixteenth note in this measure has its own importance and must be emphasized. An exact tempo in this whole passage is absolutely necessary, and the slightest carelessness in this respect would be fatal. The same applies to mm. 51–59. This section is played vivace, and one must pitch right into the new faster tempo exactly on the first beat of m. 51, without any working up towards it. It is important to give special care to observance of the punctuation.

Measures 55–59 are played staccato and playfully, with a "wiping" touch.

We now come back to the beginning (da capo), and this re-exposition may be played exactly like the first time. It is quite correct, and there is nothing wrong in doing it. Still, it is possible to obtain more variety and more coloring, by altering some of the shadings and even the pulsation and the tempo. Brahms himself shows us the way, because in the original version the first motive is brought in once more in the last section, in a frank allegro. We can bring some of this spirit into play here. May we suggest that the second time, (after the initial attack of m. 1, which must be executed once more with force and energy), the molto sostenuto and free rubato of m. 2

and following, is gradually transformed into a more rhythmic and straight delivery *at the same time* as the tempo picks up little by little, until it works directly into the vivo at m. 13. One continues then to the end, increasing steadily the vitality and the intensity of the utterance. The vision should be one of dancers who become intoxicated with the beauty of the music and the feelings which it expresses. The flashing colors of the costumes; the sort of frenzy that seizes the crowd; the exalted joy which permeates the whole celebration; all afford a fine opportunity for our imagination to take its course. Once more we refer to Emanuel Moór: "What a splendor, those nights in Hungary," he said, "when the country folks, all dressed up in their nicest garments, gather around the musicians on the village square. The violinist starts, improvising. He doesn't know what he is going to play. It comes to him on the wings of inspiration. It may be a reverie, or a love song, depending upon whether he looks at the starry sky, or at a lovely maiden. On and on he plays, changing his moods, while his companions surround him and also improvise their accompaniment, harmonies and all. And it always ends by dances, in which everyone joins. They all become frantic with excitement, and they dance, dance, until dawn."

Spirit and Atmosphere

Let us try, then, to express some of this attractive description, especially after the da capo and on to the closing chords. There, one must take great care of the way in which the "building up" is carried out. Each measure should have more intensity, volume of tone, and speed, than the preceding one; but less than the one that follows. The "let down" in mm. 19–20 and 41–42 will be also reduced to a strict minimum; more of a hint than an actual slowing down, more in the spirit than in the tempo itself.

Another important point in the interpretation of a piece calling for freedom and tempo rubato is the unity of conception. It is easy to fall into exaggeration, which would cause distortion. Each little episode and change of rhythm and tempo should be thought over carefully and in relation to the ensemble, which must retain its purity of line. Any deficiency in this respect would cause this lovely music to sound "chopped up" and incoherent. Debussy used to say that in his mind there were only two conductors who could (they still do!) play *La Mer* in a way satisfactory to him: Arturo Toscanini [1867-1957] and Bernardino Molinari [1880-1952]; because, in his own words, they treated it as a whole and as a real classical symphony, instead of turning it into a musical puzzle game by emphasizing too much the little details.

The last chords in mm. 102–103 must be played bravely, boldly, with decision, well marked and separated, with short touches of pedal which will improve the quality of the tone. Use a forearm attack, right off the keys. No ritardando whatsoever; it would create an anticlimax, and would absolutely ruin the conclusion.

It is, of course, difficult to express adequately with words the subtleness of many points when the music is, as in the present case, distinctly representative of a nation and of a race. Listening to the native Zigeuner orchestras will prove a most valuable experience; and much can be learned from their playing, since the genuine ones still retain their ancestors' secret, that singular power to evoke upon their fiddles the echoes of heroic deeds, the sighs of the lovelorn, and the glory of the reddening sunsets over the horizons of their fatherland.

HUNGARIAN DANCE No. 6

JOHANNES BRAHMS
Arranged by Maurice Dumesnil
[original four-hand version in Db major]

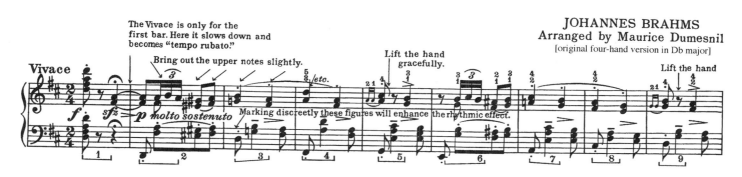

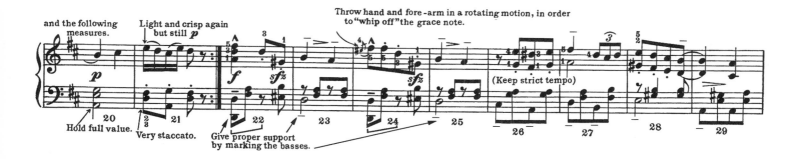

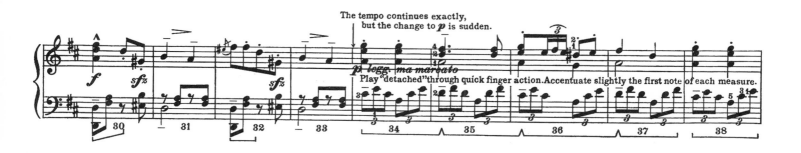

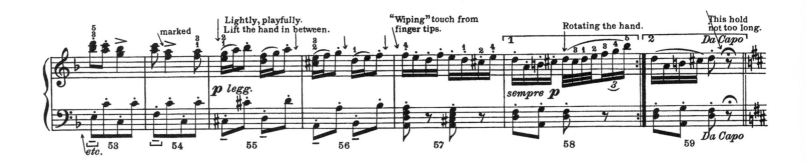

"*Autumn*"
A Master Lesson on this Famous Composition by Composer
MADAME CÉCILE CHAMINADE
[December 1930]

*A*utumn, a composition for the piano, was written long years ago. It might almost be called a youthful composition. The writer does not belong in that class of composers who disdain the compositions in their early manner. In the work of the young artist there is all the ardor of life full of illusions. There is frankness. There is spontaneity unrestrained. Also there is complete scorn of the fashion in art indeed, "fashion" cannot affect the true artist. There is, in short, all that sincerity which gives permanence to the artwork.

Autumn was written in Perigord, in the *chateau de Laforge*, the old homestead of the composer. There the writer went every year to pass the months of September and October with her family. In this beautiful wild country, full of murmuring springs, waterfalls and rivulets, the beginning of Autumn was intensely poetic. The high hills, which surrounded the property, were covered, at this season of the year, with blue lavender and pink heather. The long walks, bordered with chestnut trees centuries old, the woods of yoke-elm, with their amber colored foliage—all these invited the soul to meditation. Thus was *Autumn* inspired by this poetic setting, at this season of the year when nature is at peace, and when one lives again the beautiful days of the past—lives them over with keen regret that they are drawn to a close.

A Reflective Beginning

The first part of the composition, therefore, is a meditation in communion with nature, a meditation interrupted by a blast of wind, the precursor of stormy days to come. In the midst of the tempest, the first theme reappears far away, obscured, and then several violent startling gusts return. Finally, all the storm subsides, and the reverie returns, more calm than in the beginning, and this gentle mood is prolonged to the end.

Such is the spirit that should color the interpretation of *Autumn*.

Autumn was published in the first collection of "Concert Etudes I, Op. 35;" but really it should rather have been called a *Pièce Romantique*. The tempo is indicated by the metronome: Lento, ♪=112, but the majority of composers, and I agree with them, consider that it is next to impossible to give by means of the metronome an exact idea of the tempo which is to be sustained. Pieces which are characterized chiefly by velocity are excepted, for they have swift and decided movement. But in pieces of impassioned or romantic character one must always depend a little, even a great deal, on the intelligence and the musicianship of the interpreter who must impregnate himself with the color and the spirit of the piece which he is performing. Naturally the interpreter should begin by consulting the indications of tempo which the composer has supplied, in order to enter into the meaning of the piece as a whole, and to avoid departing too far from such suggestions of speed.

The Composer's Editing

In *Autumn* the nuances are very carefully indicated. There is, therefore, little to add concerning the interpretation, if the student consults these indications with care.

With regard to the pedal, there is something to be said, something which perhaps may cause surprise, for it marks a veritable evolution in the use of the pedal. This evolution has been apparent for some time.

The writer herself did not wait until now to adopt this new procedure. Nevertheless, it was adopted with caution. For surely there is no worse fault than that of holding the damper pedal through a succession of chords so as to confuse the musical idea and to produce cacophony. Clearness in playing is no more highly esteemed by anyone than the present writer. Therefore no one demands a more judicious use of the pedal. Nevertheless, there are impassioned passages, passages which are orchestral in character, where the natural sonority of the piano seems somewhat dry and, at times, even inadequate. In such passages the pedal is the only recourse for obtaining the required atmosphere.

For example, consider the rapid portion of *Autumn*—that strident, rapid, violent passage which imitates the tempest. If the pedal is used in the strictly logical manner, with judicious restraint, without breaking any rules of harmony, the passage will fail of the stormy effect which it demands.

Advice with Reservations

True, this advice is a little dangerous, if it is addressed to inexperienced students, for they can easily go to the opposite extreme and, falling into the habit of using too much pedal, thus produce only an incoherent jumble of sounds. But, in the present case, the advice is to be applied specially to *Autumn*, in which composition itself the pedaling is so very carefully marked that, if its directions are followed, the student will obtain the desired result.

It is necessary to have a good technic for the proper performance of *Autumn*. Oft times the interpreter, gifted with a pleasing tone and with natural charms, gives an excellent impression of the singing portion, with which the composition opens, and yet, for lack of technic, destroys all the effect of the other period. For this portion requires a sure technic and considerable strength. This is the reason why the composition is considered difficult, for, to make it effective, one must be possessed of both charm and technic.

Doubtless the writer will be informed that upon reading this opinion many well-intentioned persons, who might wish to play *Autumn*, will be deterred from the attempt. Certainly that is not the composer's intention. So, rather, the writer hopes that she may persuade the young performers that work is the precious tool without which success is impossible. Félix Le Couppey [1811-1887], famous professor at the Conservatoire and teacher of the writer, used to say that he could determine, from hearing a very simple and calm Andante, whether or not the performer possessed technic. Indeed, the sonority of tone produced by the finger which has been well trained is quite different from that of a player who is not far advanced. The roundness of tone and the legato beneath the supple pressure of the fingers give evidence of technic and of strength even in a *pianissimo* phrase.

In this age, when time moves so swiftly, when everyone hurries through everything, the thought of serious and persevering study may seem tedious, unattractive, even alarming. So it may be of some avail to recall the proverb, forever true: "Time has no respect for that which is created without his participation."

AUTUMN
ETUDE DE CONCERT
No. 2

C. CHAMINADE, Op. 35

A Master Lesson
Upon Chopin's "Aeolian Harp" Etude, Opus 25, No. 1

By Isidor Philipp

PROFESSOR OF PIANOFORTE AT THE CONSERVATOIRE

[May 1931]

Is it possible to analyze with any definiteness the magical art of a Chopin? This art which ravishes our senses, charms our intelligence, touches our heart and enters into our soul—this is something impalpable! But it cannot be denied that this music has a mysterious power, the power to awaken in us, without the help of a single word, the most divine feelings which range all the way from reverie to ecstasy, from simple submission to its charm, up to the heights of enthusiasm.

For a century and more the music of Chopin has lived—*all* his music has lived. This was a genius without equal, in that he invented everything, discovered everything. The most exquisite melodies, the most audacious harmonies—grace, tenderness, elegance, depth of meaning, beauty of form—all these different strings he possessed in his lyre. And he made them all resound with an intensity of emotion which may well be called incomparable.

A great English poet once said, "Music begins where speech leaves off." In other words, when our emotions, whatever they happen to be, reach that point at which words alone are incapable of expressing their intensity, there music is called upon to voice the depth of the feelings which dominate us. This fact has never seemed more true than when one recalls it in connection with Chopin's music.

The power to rouse the emotions which any work of art may possess arises from that work's sincerity. And as Chopin ever listened to the voice of his own heart, so his works are the very image of his passions, his longings, his sufferings. My master, George Mathias [1826-1910], was one of the best of Chopin's pupils. He used to relate many reminiscences of Chopin's talks, for Chopin had a great affection for this pupil of his.

Whatever Man Can Perform

In these Etudes will be found everything that the piano can require of an artist. There are new effects of harmony, of phrasing, to which no player, until Chopin's day, had been accustomed. There are tremendous chords, either solid or in arpeggio form. There are effects in arpeggios which demand the hands of a giant. There are combinations of thirds and of sixths; there are octaves, legato or staccato (to be joined by using the 3rd, 4th and 5th fingers or to be played from the wrist). All these effects were new. They were so original that even today these two books of Etudes are still astonishing. Never has anything exceeded them in perfection.

Chopin was very generous with his time, in giving his lessons. He was, moreover, very exacting, for teaching was to him a veritable act of priesthood. (His price for one lesson was normally one *louis d'or*.) He had the student place the hand lightly on the keys, the fingers of the right hand upon:

$$\overset{1}{E}\ \overset{2}{F\sharp}\ \overset{3}{G\sharp}\ \overset{4}{A\sharp}\ \overset{5}{B};$$

of the left hand on:

$$\overset{5}{E}\ \overset{4}{F\sharp}\ \overset{3}{G\sharp}\ \overset{2}{A\sharp}\ \overset{1}{B\sharp}.$$

The hand has a natural pose, when placed in this position, and is in a *normal* condition also, without contractions. The shorter fingers,

namely the 5th and the thumb, find a comfortable position on the white keys. The hands are turned outward a very little, almost imperceptibly.

Beauty of tone must be the immediate object of study. Every attack which made too dry a tone was excluded. The pupils of Chopin began with exercises for the five fingers. These exercises were adapted to each pupil, and increased according to the need of each.

To teach how to pass the thumb under, he used the scale of B major. This scale had to be played first in staccato, very slowly, with so much movement of the wrist as to leave the hand suspended in the air, after each note. But there must be no heaviness in this touch. The hand shifted position as the thumb passed under.

The next step, after playing the scale staccato, was to play the same scale, leaning at first on the key and holding the notes over, with the hand always held high. Next the scale was accented in twos, and finally a true legato was achieved. The same method of procedure was used for the arpeggio.

Chopin was accustomed to teach the scales in different accents, and made this exercise of much importance, for it served to correct the weakness of certain fingers. He had the scales practiced, also, with differing quantities of tone, *ff*, then *pp*, and also both slowly and quickly. To play a strong chord—he used to say—it is necessary to "concentrate" the hand, so to speak. For the opposite effect, one may even "caress" the keys with long fingers to obtain a truly "velvety" tone.

In the Etude in A-flat major (Op. 25, No. 1) he has traced a simple melody upon a filmy support of arpeggios, which are divided between the two hands. Schumann felt that this composition was a poem rather than an Etude. He has said that the playing of Chopin made him think of an Aeolian harp, and, without doubt, this impression was suggested by the Etude in A-flat major. One of Chopin's pupils is responsible for the tradition that the Master described this Etude as "a picturesque vision of a little herdsman who through wind and rain piped his melody, in the shelter of a cave." A particularly charming passage in this Etude is the original modulation, in the very middle of the Etude, which transposes a phrase into *A major*. Here, too, one is especially impressed with Chopin's fine sense of sonority and the great delicacy of treatment. It is plain that Chopin could not conceive of an Etude in the dry technical sense, as something adapted to technical work alone, no matter how transcendent the technic itself might be.

One must study first the melody, to give it sonority and mellowness in the attack with the 5th finger. Throughout the whole Etude one must think of sonority. The student should work over sections of sixteen measures at a time, holding each note as long as possible.

Play very slowly, and *forte*. Use at first the fingering 4 2 3 1 2 3 throughout and afterward 5 3 4 2 3 4 throughout. After much practice in this manner, use the regular fingering, but with the nuances: *f, p, pp,* each in turn.

If these ways of practicing do not result in the ideal lightness which is necessary, the student should have recourse to various

accents as: 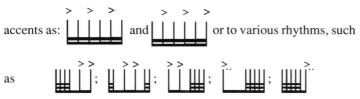 or to various rhythms, such

as

The left hand, which is very difficult, ought to be practiced thus:

and then with the same rhythms which have been indicated for the right hand.

It will be useful, also, to transpose the Etude into A major, using the same fingering that has been used in A flat.

A word may be said also as to the way of holding the hands in this adorable work. They should be held rather high and as if they "had no bones," and the arms must be absolutely free and supple. Do not forget, at the 39th measure, the original fingering, invented by Georges Mathias:

—the thumb on F—a fingering which gives an exquisite softness to this note.

Piano Lessons with Camille Saint-Saëns
By Isidor Philipp
[July 1934]

Saint-Saëns [1835-1921] was fifty-four years of age when I first had the privilege of meeting him. I was eighteen years old when Stephen Heller [1813-1888] gave me a word of introduction. One morning soon after, I armed myself with all my courage, and, trembling, rang at his door. At that time he lived at 14, rue Monsieur le Prince, in a modest apartment, very simply furnished. That day he seemed anxious, preoccupied, but he received me with great kindness.

"You are timid," he said. "That is a serious fault in an artist. I was timid, too. Come, play me something!"

I sat down at the piano and began the first movement of Sonata, Op. 53, of Beethoven. He heard it through without stirring. Then, "Something else," he said. "Have you any Mendelssohn?"

I played the *Rondo Capriccioso*.

"*That* is very good," was his verdict. "Come again. Come Friday at nine o'clock. Your playing is promising. You interest me. Don't be so timid."

The first lesson, which lasted from nine o'clock till noon (and the Master kept me to luncheon), was somewhat stormy. Wrath, remonstrance, encouragement—I endured them all with joy. Madame Saint-Saëns, his charming mother, who heard him raging and scolding, came into the room several times.

"It is nothing," he said, "only that this animal is too timid." But I, I was happy. . . .

The Gauntlet of Criticism

Chopin, Liszt, Schumann were as familiar to him as the older classics. He had curiosity for all music and was eager to know the latest compositions. His memory was stupendous. His mind was so clear, vivid and exact that the clearness and swiftness of his criticism compelled the student to understand and to make progress. Saint-Saëns did not pass over in silence a single mistake. He was extremely impatient. Often, after scolding and reproaching, he would leave the room, slamming the door behind him. Then his mother would

bring him back, and the lesson would begin again.

After returning from my lessons I wrote down religiously the advice which he gave me and some of these maxims follow:

"The mania for too rapid *tempi*, which is so prevalent in our day, destroys the form of the music and makes it degenerate into a noise, confused and uninteresting. Nothing remains but speed and that is not enough."

"No composition for the piano will ever be well written, no playing of the piano will ever be interesting, unless the bass is made just as important as the melody."

"The two hands must function at the same instant and not one after the other, as is too often the case. Sometimes this error is due to mere carelessness, sometimes to the idea that thus the execution has more grace and charm—which is a great mistake and leads only to affectation and mannerisms."

"It is only the study of tone (*sonorité*) which makes the piano interesting."

"To abuse the pedal is odious. But it can be used very often without abuse. At first it should be omitted as far as possible, in practicing. Then, in working with it, one should remember that its variety of effects must never bring about confusion."

He was a teacher of the first rank—very exacting concerning matters of technic, purity of execution, study of tone, of the quality of sound, of pianistic color, of phrasing, of just accents, of the style appropriate to each composer. (He often illustrated from his piano, for, as I have said, he carried all the music in his head.) Besides insisting upon all these matters, he took pleasure in opening the mind of the pupil to whatever was truly worthy of interest, and drew his attention to other arts besides that of music.

To me he was a clairvoyant, guide and an incomparable friend.

["Aeolian Harp" Etude]

Allegro sostenuto M. M. ♩=104

FR. CHOPIN, Op.25, No.1

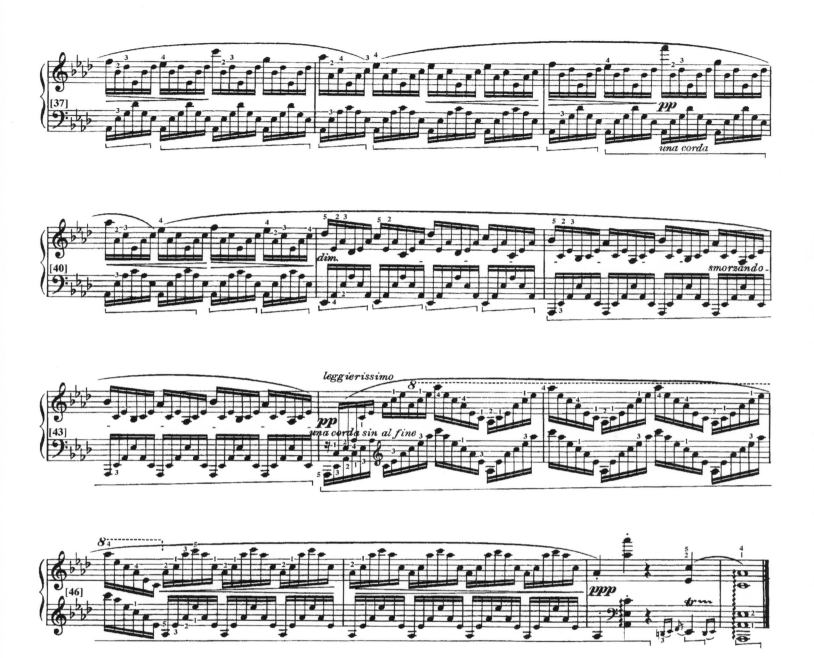

A Master Lesson by Mark Hambourg
ON THE NOCTURNE IN F-SHARP MAJOR, OP. 15, NO. 2, OF CHOPIN

The Eminent Russo-Anglian Virtuoso Pianist, hailed all over Europe as "The Modern Rubinstein," presents an exceptional study of a great masterpiece

[September 1935]

The name *nocturne* was first used by the composer and pianist, John Field [1782-1837], to denote a quiet, reflective kind of pianoforte piece. Its original meaning was a sort of serenade, and it was thus employed by Mozart. But John Field, by giving to four or five lovely idyllic compositions of his own the name of nocturne, established the title as a popular one for this type of pianoforte work. Field's nocturnes were intimate poems of grace and charm without oversentimentality, and Chopin, who later immortalized the nocturne by the exquisite pieces he wrote under this title, owes much to Field who prepared the way for him. For Chopin's nocturnes embody much the same kind of emotion, the same form of melody, and the same delicate embroideries on the themes, which characterize, on the lesser plane, the charming Lyrics of [John] Field. It is interesting to note that Chopin himself used to recommend Field's nocturnes to his pupils for the study of good singing tone.

Schumann called Chopin "the boldest [and] proudest poetic spirit" of his time [*NZM*, 1839]. Certainly as a composer for the pianoforte he stands in a world by himself, as an inventor of fascinating rhythms, haunting romantic melodies, of magic harmonies, and delightful sentiment.

Every Tone to Sing

In his teaching of pupils Chopin seemed to lay most stress on the importance of touch, and would declare that everything in his compositions must be played with a singing tone; the passage-work as well as the melodies, and equally so, the bass and the inner parts.

With regard to the fact that so many players nowadays allow themselves great license in the use of *tempo rubato* when rendering Chopin's works, it is instructive to know that he himself used a metronome while practicing, and did not encourage emotional distortions of the rhythms of his works. "The singing hand," he said, "may trespass on the time, but the accompanying one must keep to it." He would liken the music to a tree whose branches are swayed by the wind. The trunk of the tree, he would say, is the steady time, the moving leaves are the inflections of the melody."

Some Technical Helps

We are considering here the Nocturne in F-sharp major, which was an early work of Chopin, published in 1834 and dedicated to his friend Hiller. It opens with a simple, joyous melody which, however, is soon elaborated with all kinds of graceful embellishments, and these embellishments Chopin seems to weave with ever increasing subtlety each time the fancy strikes him.

The beginning of this nocturne, in fact the whole of the first part of the work up to m. 25, should be played with flexible rhythm and with the embellishments of the melody introduced with restrained rubato effects. These embroideries (if I may call them so) must be played gracefully, without hurrying over them, the endeavor being to give the feeling of portamento from one note to another, where the phrase demands it, in the same manner as a good singer would sing such ornaments to his song.

The melody, itself, must be rendered with a singing tone, and with strict attention given to the rise and fall of the melodic line. It is also most important not to forget to support the melody, throughout, with the bass accompaniment, to which must be imparted a warm quality of sound, thus making it a satisfactory framework for the lovely song and its constant ornamentations.

The *Nocturne* starts in *mezzo piano* tone with a gentle decrescendo on the first beat of m. 1, and another one (always keeping the music *piano*) [after] the third beat of m. 2. In m. 4, where there is an eighth-note on the third beat in the treble, a slight pause just a little more marked should be made after this note, as though taking a breath.

Another pause just a little more marked should be made on the second eighth-note, F$\sharp$, in the treble in m. 6; in fact this pause should amount to a definite though slight, fermata on the F$\sharp$, before proceeding to the next note. The trill on the second beat in m. 7, in the treble, must have a small accent; and the trill itself must not be played too fast. In m. 8, on the second eighth note of the second beat, where a little ornament leads back again into the first theme, this ornament and the chord in the left hand, on which it is based, must be played with a full tone; and a slight breath pause should be made after the chord on C$\sharp$ which precedes it, whilst the A$\sharp$, a dotted sixteenth-note on the second half of the second beat, must be played lingeringly.

We Seek the Soul

Coming to m. 12, there should be a small ritardando in the beginning of the measure, with a return to tempo in the second part of it. A crescendo, leading up to the sforzando on the high F$\sharp$ in the treble, should be observed in m. 14; and the tone should sink again to *mezzo forte* at the end of the following measure. The last note in the bass of m. 15, which is a B$\natural$, should be played by the right hand, in conjunction with the G$\sharp$ in the treble, for the sake of smoothness of execution.

A new phrase starts in the right hand, on the last half of the second beat in m. 16; and this must be rendered in a sadder mood than the first bright subject. Also, until m. 21, the tempo should be somewhat slower. In mm. 22 and 23 the music should return to the original tempo, and the sextuplet figure on the second beat of m. 22 should be brought out with suppressed passion, whilst from there onwards to m. 24 the tempo should accelerate with growing emotion. In m. 24 a ritardando on the reiterated A$\sharp$s in the right hand, on the second beat of the measure, leads into m. 25, where we arrive at the most difficult part of the Nocturne, which is marked Doppio Movimento. (Doppio Movimento means the same metronomic length of beat, but with the notes of two of the former beats pressed into one of the new ones.)

The Spirit Charges

Here occurs a change in the character of the music; and the happy song which fills the first part of the piece disappears. In its place we now have a restless invocation which increases in intensity and yearning until m. 42, when it gradually dies down again and sinks away into m. 48. The Doppio Movimento is extremely difficult to play correctly, owing to the cross rhythms in the right hand. The lower part of the music for the right hand is in figures of five sixteenth-notes, which must fit in with the two-four time of the melody imposed upon it from above, whilst the bass also is in syncopation with the treble as a whole.

The first eight measures of the Doppio Movimento must be played in equal groups of five, in the running sixteenth-note figures in the right hand, the melody being well brought out above it, and the passing notes in the melody being played very lightly.

In order to master successfully the difficulty of this Doppio Movimento, we will here give five different ways of practicing it, each of which should be studied with care. These should be found very helpful in mastering the technical problems of this part of the composition. First we study the melody, with the right hand:

and so on, in octaves only. Then this figuration:

and so on, bringing out the melody from above. And then:

and so on, bringing out the melody from below. Follow this with:

and so on, holding the melody in octaves and practicing the middle figures for the development of articulation. And then:

and so on, practicing with a staccato touch.

In the first eight measures of the Doppio Movimento, the chords which appear on the second half of each beat of each measure for the left hand, must strike just after the third note of the quintuple sixteenth-note figure in the right hand, so that the bass chord sounds in between the third and fourth notes of the quintuplet. Similarly, the last eighth-note in each measure of the bass, should strike just after the third sixteenth-note of the second quintuplet.

In m. 33 the rhythm becomes definitely divided into twos and threes, instead of fives, and the chords on the second half of the first beat and on the last half of the second beat, in the bass, are struck together with the first note of the triplet figures in the right hand on these same beats.

I keep the tone soft throughout m. 33, and I play with markedly strict rhythm the thirty-second notes which begin to elaborate further the figures from m. 33 onward in the right hand. In m. 36 there occur the notes C♮ and B in both hands. These notes are two eighth-notes in the left hand, and two sixteenth-notes in the right hand; and each must be accented and brought out in imitation one of the other. In m. 37 begins a gradual crescendo, and the melody should make a slight pause after the last note of m. 38, which is C♯ in the right hand, before attacking in *forte* tone the octave D♮ on the first beat of m. 39. This pause is merely a device, which I have pointed out before, like taking a breath when singing, to make more effective the *forte* note which follows the pause.

The *forte* continues with increasing volume and passion until it reaches its zenith in the *fortissimo* of m. 41; and then it begins to die down again from the middle of m. 42 and finally reaches a *pianissimo* in the second half of m. 46. Here, on the second beat of the measure, on the bass octave D♮ in the right hand, there should be made a little pause—lingering on the notes, as if loth to let them go. The reiterated D♮s on the first and second beats of the treble in m. 44 should be accented; also the A♮ in the broken chord in the bass of the same measure, and on the first beat of m. 45, [on the octave D♮] in the right hand; and the E in the bass chord of the same beat.

And Calm Returns

The Doppio Movimento trails away into nothing, in m. 48; and it ends with a fermata or pause. The burst of emotion is spent, and the happy lyrical melody resumes its graceful way, embellished by ever more elaborate ornamentations.

The cascade of notes in the right hand of m. 51 should start with slight accents on the first, fourth and seventh notes; namely, B♮, A♯, and A♮, with a little pause on the twentieth note, D♮, and on the thirty-fifth note, A♯. These accents and pauses are used to give shape to the whole passage of notes.

In m. 55 an accent must be given on the trill in the treble; and the whole measure should be played rubato, but unexaggerated and with a little melancholy. On the second half of the first beat in m. 57, where the ornamentation starts on G♯ in the treble, a portamento should be made between the G♯ and the preceding E♯, the fourth finger on E♯ giving an impression as of sliding up to the next note. At the end of this ornamentation a rallentando must be made, and the last two notes of this m. 57 should be stressed in both hands. The tempo must be resumed on the first note of m. 58, and the bass in this measure and the following one should be made to sound as much as possible like the muted brass instruments in an orchestra—very distinct, yet muffled and mysterious.

An Eloquent Diminuendo

Each first note of the descending figures in the right hand mm. 58 and 59 must be stressed; namely, the B on the last half of the second beat in m. 58, and the G♯, D♯, B, and G♯ in m. 59.

In m. 60, on the third and fourth sextuplet figures, there should be a slight decrescendo, then crescendo up to the first note of the fourth sextuplet. This gentle rising and falling of the tone should continue in the similar figure in m. 61, until the end of this measure where each of the notes in the last sextuplet should be slightly emphasized. The last note in m. 61 of the right hand, which is a C♯, should be held a little longer than the others and be given the effect of sliding up to the final A♯ in the treble, like an accomplished singer, or a fine violinist, would make a portamento in the ending of such a phrase.

The whole of the last five measures, with the exquisite descending triplet and sextuplet passages in the right hand, must be played tenderly and with skillfully decreasing tone, until in m. 61 it has become faint, almost to nothing, yet still with the rhythm distinct and the outlines of the sextuplets clearly defined so that the emphasis on the last six notes falls naturally into the tone scheme. These final measures, in fact, should create the impression of the gradual falling of the curtain over an eloquent stage scene.

NOCTURNE

All embellishments should be played gracefully and unhurriedly

FR. CHOPIN, Op. 15, No. 2

A Master Lesson on Chopin's Military Polonaise in A-Major

By the Famous Polish Pianist and Composer

SIGISMUND STOJOWSKI

[February 1926]

The Importance and Nature of Rhythm

In the beginning there was rhythm. . . . From the "revolutions of celestial orbs," the countless vibrations of distant and mysterious ether, through the tidal motions in the vasty deeps of oceans wide, down to the heart-throbs of suffering and struggling humanity, even to the life-drawing breaths of the lowliest creatures, rhythm seems the very essence and mainspring of being. Without that all-governing principle of order, the Cosmos would be mere chaos. And, wherever the rhythmic pulse ceases to beat, life ceases to flow. "Manifestation of the relentless energy of the universe," as Paderewski once put it, rhythm includes two elements: a *dynamic* moment, the *affirmation*, as it were, of Life through beat and accent, within time and meter, in accordance with the *cyclic* principle of recurrence, repetition, rotation, to which all phenomena conform in their endless diversity and which the mind conceives as law and order.

Man and his art are subject to the universal law. Music—whether it be that of the spheres or simply that which bursts forth in song from man's breast—is indeed inseparable from and inconceivable without rhythm in its dual aspect. In the propelling, dynamic urge of rhythm lies Music's emotional appeal. And what we have come to call musical form is but an extension of the rhythmic principle of order and proportion, which raises the Art to the plane of intellectual perception and achievement. By virtue of rhythm the heart's outcry crystallizes into Art. In his desire to perpetuate himself, his Gods and heroes, man moulds his ideas and their deeds into patterns of verse. So, too, the craving for liberty that dwells in man's breast prompts him to devise gestures, steps and mimicry as a self-imposed rhythmic discipline, which is Dance. No less than language, dance is a faithful mirror of racial and national psychology. From the languid or frantic evolutions and contortions of semi-savage tribes, to the elaborately skillful graces of a highly polished society, from "sword-dance" to minuet, from *The Lord of Salisbury's his Pavin* [from *Parthenia,* 1613, Orlando Gibbons, 1583-1625] to some foxtrot or tango born on modern America's "Barbary Coast"—there are differences in time and latitude, mood and temper, taste and education. Yet, the fundamental impulse remains the same, attested by patterns crude or noble, simple or complex, but rich and varied like humanity itself.

The Dances of Poland

"Le Pologne Dansante" (Dancing Poland)—as a Frenchman defined the nation, was no misnomer. Poland's originality asserted itself since the dawn of history by remarkable inventiveness in rhythmic patterns which have survived in a treasury of folk-songs and fertilized the national musical crop. Rhythms, like all vibrations, are communicative, not to say infectious.

Grave or gay, full of vim or solemnly dignified, the manifold strains, changing moods and shifting accents of Polish popular dances faithfully mirror a people ardent, chivalrous and brave, passionate, capricious and moody, enamored of pomp, panoply and bright colors, yet prone to sentiment and reverie, in fact easily carried from extreme joy and enthusiasm to the opposite pole of sadness and despondency. Like the moods reflected, the patterns are infinitely varied. Triple rhythms mostly predominate and syncopations are plentiful. It is through the position of accents as well as in general character that the dances are differentiated and recognizable. The Polonaise which achieved such universal vogue, as contrasted with the more regional Mazovienne, or Mazurkam, equally in triple time, moves more slowly and solemnly, in stately and dignified fashion, though it is by no means lacking in fire and energy. Its main rhythmic accent mostly coincides with the metric one, placed as it is on the first beat, which gives to it its peculiar march-like character. Even so, it does not elude the capricious Polish shifting of accents, occasionally emphasizing the second beat, as, for instance, in every second measure at the beginning of the Trio in Chopin's A-Major Polonaise, which we will presently discuss. This may have misguided [James] Huneker [1857-1921] into the belief that the characteristic accent of the Polonaise regularly falls on the second beat.[1] Again, the third beat assumes a peculiar significance in cadences. The Polonaise has developed, in phrase structure, a typical cadence of its own, a graceful melodic curve, winding up by a stop or ornamental turn on the second degree of the scale descending upon the tonic, comparable to the feminine ending in poetry.

We may add to these features that of a frequently used pulsating accompaniment of which Chopin was excessively fond, though it remained for Liszt to make of it an almost abusive use (Trio of the E major Polonaise). We refer to the well-known rhythmic patterns:

The Origin of the Polonaise and Its Place In National Life

The origin of the Polonaise, like all origins, is more or less obscure. One of the early Chopin biographers, Karasowski [Dresden, 1877], relates that after the Polish nobility had elected Prince Henri de Valois to the throne of Poland (1574), a reception was given to the French prince upon his arrival, at the royal castle in Warsaw, when the Polish nobles defiled with their wives before the new king in a fashion reminiscent of the solemn French Pavane, but to strains of wholly different native Polish music. This story has led to the erroneous belief that the Polonaise was born right there and then. Nor is the inference, possibly drawn by some "authorities" from the same source, that the Polonaise is but a tributary of, or still worse, a mere caricature of the wholly different French Pavane, anything but a gratuitous assumption. The Polonaise may, on that occasion, have made its first appearance at court, the ceremonial of which it was steadily to accompany ever since. In its inception,

---

[1][All references to Huneker in this article are from *Chopin; The Man and His Music*, Dover, p. 182].

however, it was not an imported and courtly dance, but distinctly native and popular. Its characteristic rhythms and cadences are implicit in many folk-songs of ancient origin and this writer has not hesitated to use its freely adapted pattern in some choral settings of old Polish Christmas Carols, such as the well-known "W żobie leży" (In the Manger He lies).

It remains true, nevertheless, that in the course of time the Polonaise became appropriated by the gentry with whom it grew institutional, so to speak, and inseparable from all festive occasions, while the peasants more faithfully favored the livelier dances of the Mazurka type. In fact, as the peasant garb to this very day seems a requisite of the boisterous and jolly Mazurka, so the "Kontusz" (long frock-coat) falling clown to the knees with its peculiar floating sleeves, the richly adorned feathered-caps, colored high boots, the whole brilliant attire of the gentry seems inseparably identified with the Polonaise's festive pageant. "A vivid pageant of martial splendor," writes Huneker, "at once the symbol of war and love, a weaving, cadenced, voluptuous dance." "The Polonaise," says Franz Liszt, "is the true and purest type of Poland's national character." [*Life of Chopin*, Ch. 2] But eloquent as is Liszt's description of it, one must turn to Poland's national poet, Mickiewicz, whose great epic, "Pan Tadeusz," is now available to the English speaking world in a beautiful prose translation [by George Rapall Noyes, 1917], in order to form an adequate idea of the true character and the place which the Polonaise held in national life. To quote but briefly,

> "The Chamberlain stepped forward and lightly throwing back the flowing sleeves of his Kontusz and twirling his moustache, he offered his arm to the bride. With a polite bow he invited her to lead off in the first couple . . .
>
> And the couples followed one another merrily and uproariously . . .
>
> The circle would disperse and then contract once more! As when an immense serpent winds into a thousand folds, so there was seen a perpetual change amid the gay, parti-colored garments of the ladies, the gentlemen and the soldiers, like glittering scales gilded by the beams of the western sun and relieved against the dark pillows of turf. Brisk was the dance and loud the music . . ."

Chopin's Polonaise in A-Major

It was some vision like the above which terrified, haunted and inspired Chopin on the Island of Majorca, possibly amid the walls of the convent of Valombrosa, in the wake of some sleepless night of meditation, reminiscence of bygone days and creative effort. The already ailing Chopin was seeking relief there in 1839 in company of George Sand. The two Polonaises published a year later as Op. 40 belong to that most fruitful period when Chopin had reached the height of his genius. Think of the music-lovers of the day able to secure as primaries in that blessed year: the Sonata in B-flat minor, the Second Impromptu, second Ballade, Scherzo in C-sharp minor, Op. 39, four Mazurkas, Op. 41, the Valse, Op. 47, and the two Polonaises mentioned! The richness of the composer's fancy as well as the pliability of his chosen form are wonderfully illustrated by these twin companions of Op. 40, the Polonaises in A-major and C-minor. While deeply contrasted, they seem complementary of one another; brothers in mould, they are each other's opposites in mood. Between themselves, they indeed epitomize the whole tale of "Poland's glory" and "Poland's downfall." They seem to reflect not merely subjective impressions but collective aspirations and experiences. Contrary to the theory propounded that only the major mode is fit to translate collective feelings, the fact being adduced in proof that all national anthems are in a major key, the writer feels that the deep pathos of the C-minor Polonaise indeed transcends personal emotion and seems to voice the grief and woe of an entire people. But to none of Chopin's Polonaises does the appellation of "heroic hymns of battle" better apply than to the A-major. Because of its martial ring, it is popularly labelled the "Military Polonaise." Performers beware, however, lest this does not turn into a sad travesty, if it be made to evoke the rigidity and stiffness of some Prussian drill-sergeants! Nor is it necessary to make it symbolic of some cavalry charge storming a difficult position at top-speed. It is not speed but fire and power that matter. Huneker is justly surprised that this Polonaise should be so much played while being so very "muscular." Perhaps it is the total absence of ornamental passage-work that deceives people as to its facility of execution and beguiles amateurs as well as brass-bands into hurrying through it. In truth, it demands wrists of steel and iron fingers. One is reminded of a contemporary's surprise at a handshake of Chopin's, at the "bony resistance" of this velvety hand and of Louis Enault's judicious comment about Chopin: "a frail man born to be strong" and "the skeleton of a soldier covered by feminine flesh." Huneker is right in asserting that Chopin "had the warrior in him," for indeed "there are moments when he discards gloves and deals blows that reverberate with formidable clangor." Sustained power is no easy task. For that reason—besides some esthetic considerations—it should be remembered that even the most powerful *forte* is susceptible of alternatives of relaxation and tension, of more or less accented tonal and rhythmic values, of proper distribution of light and shade, or to use a word discredited in the political world, the right "balance of power." A detailed survey will bring home the realization of this point almost at every turn.

Structural Analysis and Hints for Performance

A perfect balance between technic and expression, form and contents was certainly achieved by Chopin. His constructive ability—for a long time often underrated and but recently fully appreciated—admirably knew how to adapt form to subject-matter. With unerring instinct he discriminated between old patterns to be retained and new ones to be created in order to meet fully the requirements of the fundamental idea. A prodigious innovator, he could be wholly conservative. For a truly bold and independent spirit does not rejoice in revolution for its own sake. Genius is frequently content with filling familiar old vases with rich new wine of its own. Thus is Chopin in his Polonaise. In a great epic like the A-flat Major Polonaise (Op. 53) the dance-form becomes enriched and renovated by a novel harmonic scheme, by episodes intertwined of different color, rounded out by Introduction and Coda. The fantastic drama of the F-Sharp minor Polonaise (Op. 44) actually bursts the whole frame asunder by its curious decorative interpolations and the superimposed vision of a Mazurka. But in the A-major, this fiery outburst of concentrated energy where all is light, sound and power, the unity of mood demanded extreme simplicity as well as regularity of structure. This triumphal paean adopts the old pattern of the dance-song with its tripartite, cyclic arrangement, **A + B + A**, wherein **B**—the Trio—brings a new idea in a related key (the subdominant in this case) while **A** opens and closes the cycle without resorting to either introduction, transition or coda. Each section, in turn, consists of two parts, the second but a derivation of the first and repeating the same first part so as again to reproduce on a smaller scale the tripartite scheme of the whole. Regular metric structure, elemental rhythm and dynamics, simple though rich harmony, are made to enhance the essential oneness and directness of appeal.

The initial phrase sets out boldly with the tonic chord on the strong beat of the measure, underlined by the pedal. Chopin's sarcastic comment [in a letter to Matuszynski, 1830] about [Sigismond] Thalberg [1812-1871], "a pianist who makes his shadings with his feet instead of his fingers," need not be taken too literally but should be remembered in working out with the wrist and fingers, and without pedal, the crescendo in the onrush of the five sixteenths to the accent on the first beat of the second measure. In that second measure, the triplet and the following eighths of the third beat are suggestive of percussion instruments, a rhythmic feature to come out clear and crisp, without pedal, to relieve by short staccato the strain of sustained power. The fourth measure starts with a handful of notes in extended positions the consequence being a loss of power to the accented top-note. To remedy this, the writer recommends the following for facility:

By a sudden 6/4 chord the fifth measure switches off into the key of C-sharp major. Its triplet of chords sounds peculiarly "military" with their brassy ring. But, on the last C-sharp major chord, the second eighth of the second beat, the firm grip must be somewhat relaxed to render the crescendo of the following ascent possible, while the pedal may come down again on the third beat—the melodic and chordal progressions in this high register being quite immune from blurring. These cues should be consistently observed for effective cooperation of touch and pedal. In the sixth measure—to give one more instance of proper economy of strength—the six sixteenths in octaves of both hands upon C♯ should be started *piano* and with a fresh pedal. In m. 7, a series of first inversions of perfect triads beginning with the minor triad of B, swiftly turns back to the initial key in which the eighth measure exhibits the typical cadence already described.

The second part of section **A** boldly starts with a dominant seventh of the key of E. It is, as has been said, subsidiary and derivative, bringing back some previously heard features such as the chord triplets, the six sixteenths in repeated octaves, and requiring the same mode of treatment. As strength is liable to wane, the repetitions at least in the bass, may be avoided thus:

Notice how skillfully Chopin contrives, by using several minor triads before, to turn the high light upon the major key of G♯ in which the subsidiary motive luminously reappears, a major third higher up. Quite suddenly again, and by a modulation analogous to that used at the close of the first part, the distant new key is switched back to E, whence a brief but beautiful sequential transition bridges over the resumption of the entire initial phrase.

The Trio

The Trio provides not so much a contrast as a continuation through new material. While in the accompaniment the characteristic pattern, ♪♫ ♩♫♫ prevails, the melody suggests a trumpet call. Broad

and powerful, it seems to sound the high note of a battle-cry for freedom! The call is repeated twice and strong fingers must be used to make it ring. Chopin himself is supposed to be the inventor of a proceeding—thumb and second finger joined to strike simultaneously the key—which might prove an excellent solution, though it is not devoid of danger when it comes to the quick skip of a fourth in every second measure. After this danger-point, a sudden **p**, and, like some eager response from the crowd to the preceding call, surges a sequential climax to be carefully graded until we reach, through chromatic octaves, by contrary motion in both hands, the return of the main theme scored for full orchestra. (The upper part of the right hand octaves and the lower of the left should be carefully fingered—with fourth finger on black keys and the third on A♯ of the right and on F♯ of the left—and practiced separately, legato and *pianissimo*. Another interruption with the *piano* effect of a distant key and another sequential rise, by diatonic steps in the harmony, carries us up to the familiar cadence at the end of this part.

The second part of the Trio includes a mainly dynamic and rhythmic interpolation before the resumption of the theme of the first part. Kettledrum rolls and rhythmic pulsations alternate, become condensed, and lead back to the beginning by the mighty unison of left hand octaves and right hand trills. Because of this character, we are not averse to a modified disposition of the hands, especially in the initial measure, as used by some virtuosos, for the sake of greater power, such as the following:

This enables even amateurs to make a "big row" at a comparatively small cost, provided the repetitions be quick enough in both hands to give sufficient density to the trill and adequate intensity to the crescendo. In spite of exceptional passages like this, it remains understood that Chopin's wonderfully idiomatic scoring for the piano should not be tampered with. But, since we mention slight alterations to the letter, justifiable only inasmuch as the spirit remains preserved, I will call attention to the fact that we may, at the very close of the piece, follow with impunity Mr. Paderewski's example in adding the low octave of the fundamental as a grace-note to the last beat, thus bringing the whole cycle described to a decisively conclusive stop.

POLONAISE

F. CHOPIN, Op.40, No.1

Lesson on Chopin's Polonaise in A-Flat, Op. 53

A Master Lesson by the Great Russian Virtuoso

Mark Hambourg

[December 1928]

Chopin is a unique figure in the musical world, in that he confined his genius and his interests to one instrument alone, the pianoforte. He understood its possibilities to perfection, he wrote for it with a wealth of charm and a variety of fantasy unequalled by any other composer for this instrument, and he seems to have found in it an ideal media for his creative faculty.

The Chopin Myths

The tradition about both his playing and his music, that they excel essentially on the sentimental side and by a kind of sweet efficiency, is to my mind a mistaken one, which tends to detract unfairly from the measure of his greatness. Schumann was the best advised when he described Chopin himself and his compositions as "sweetness combined with strength." For, though it is to a certain extent true that Chopin exercised his art most successfully in an atmosphere of Paris salons, amongst ecstatic ladies, still Liszt and others of his distinguished contemporary fellow-artists declared that, when he was playing at his best, he produced a noble and powerful sound from the piano, and that then often his ideas would seem too great for him to be able adequately to express. At such times he would transport hearers by the grandeur and exuberance of his delivery. Also in some of his finest works, such as the F-Minor Ballade, the Sonata in B-minor, and the Polonaise in A-flat, which I am about to consider in this article, he evinces a virility of inspiration, and depth of passion, which prove that his mentality was truly capable of the highest flights of imagination and power.

Some of the most delightful examples of Chopin's music are those of his works which typify national dance rhythms such as the Polonaises. These express preeminently the Polish spirit of romantic chivalry, and, under Chopin's magic imagination, they develop into poetic fantasies, inspired, elegant, stirring. Our present Polonaise in A-flat, Op. 53, sometimes bears the title of "The Heroic," and there is an anecdote associated with it that when Chopin played it through for the first time the room seemed to him to fill with the spectres of the warriors he had evoked (for the Polonaise in A-flat is a true war song) and that he rushed away, struck with terror, before the creations of his own fancy!

A Grand Entrance

The composition opens majestically and ponderously in an atmosphere of suppressed excitement. In m. 2, a decided accent must be given to the quarter-note chord on the third beat. In the third measure the running sixteenth note figure, starting on the second beat in both hands, should commence somewhat slowly, and increase in tone on the third beat of the measure, grow faster on the first beat of m. 4, and reduce speed again on the second and third beats of this measure, with another crescendo, culminating in an accent on the sforzando chord on the first beat of m. 5. The similar figure, commencing a tone higher on the second beat of m. 7, must be treated in a corresponding manner. In m. 10 there is an accent on the last beat and the chord on this beat and the following one should be heavy in tone.

The figure commencing on the second beat of m. 13 in the right hand should give an impression of weighty dignity; whilst the staccato octaves in the left hand must sound like a scale passage played by trombones and end with an accent on the top note of the passage, namely, on D♭ which occurs on the first beat in the bass in m. 14. Accents should be given also on the other two octaves in the bass in this measure, on the second and third beats.

The Main Theme

The lower notes of the sixteenth-note groups, which continue throughout mm. 15 and 16, should slow down about the second beat of m. 16, to prepare for the entry of the main martial and triumphal theme, which opens *a tempo* in m. 17. The dotted eighth notes on the first beat in the treble in m. 17 should be held a trifle over their value, and a slight breath pause should be made before attacking the sixteenth-notes which follow, in order to emphasize the lilt of the rhythm. In m. 19, the last eighth-note chord on the second half of the third beat must have an accent, also the subsequent three eighth-note chords in the beginning of m. 20. There should be accents on the first octave sixteenth-note of each of the descending groups of four in m. 23, and also on the trills on the second and third beats in m. 25.

At m. 26 the first four sixteenth-notes in the treble should be well brought out, with a little crescendo in tone, whilst in m. 29 there are accents to be made on the second half of the second beat, and the second half of the third beat on the sixteenth-note chords, with a slight ritardando in tempo, leading to the cadenza scale in m. 30 which must also commence with an accent on the first note, A♮, in both hands, and then proceed upwards with a tremendous crescendo. The last beat of m. 32 should then be retarded a little in tempo in order to take the theme up again in m. 33 with increased zest and power.

The next ten measures are a repetition of the main subject as introduced in m. 17, only an octave higher and somewhat elaborated. They should be treated in the same manner. At m. 43, there are the following notes to be found, namely sixteenth-note G, the first note of the sixteenth-note group on the second beat in the right hand, and A♭, the first note on the third beat of the same measure in the treble, which must both be specially brought out.

In m. 48, where the first subject closes for the moment, there should be a break in tone after the staccato chord on the first beat of the measure, and the other three chords in this measure are then attacked with great vigor, the top note of the chord in the treble on the second beat of the measure, namely, B♭, being taken by the left hand, to give it more significant utterance. In m. 49, there should be accents on the third note of the first beat in the middle parts which are thirty-second-note Cs, and also on the notes to which they lead, which are D♭ eighth-notes on the first half of the second beat in both hands.

Martial Features

Similar accents should be introduced on each of the rhythmical progressions which succeed each other throughout mm. 49 and 50, while the tempo gradually accelerates until it reaches m. 57, when it steadies down again. Meanwhile, the rhythmical figure in octaves for the left hand in the treble clef, in m. 51, should be made to sound like a trumpet call. The thirty-second-note progression, commencing on the second half of the first beat in m. 52, must be played in strict time, with accents on the two octave eighth-notes on the third beat of this measure.

Measures 53 and 54 have accents on the notes of the rhythmical progressions in the middle parts given in the same manner as in mm. 49 and 50. In m. 55 the trumpet-like figure occurs again, in the left hand, as in m. 51, and must be emphasized.

In m. 56, accents should be made on the chord on the second half of the first beat, and the second-half of the second beat, with a ritardando of tempo, to enable more emphasis to be brought to the sostenuto notes in m. 57 which must ring out proudly in the right hand, the rhythmical accompaniment in the left hand being also brought out with stirring tone. In m. 60 the four sixteenth-notes on the third beat in the right hand should be given with a singing quality of tone, and the tempo eased; but they should return to time again in the following measures. The trills in the treble, in mm. 63 and 64, can be broadened out and the tempo be here slightly retarded; whilst accents should accompany the three last chords in the bass, in m. 64.

Rhythmical Life

In the first phrase in the treble in m. 65, the rhythmic feature can be intensified (as was the case previously, in m. 17), by holding the first dotted eighth-notes a fraction of time over their proper value and then making a break or breath pause in the tone, before attacking the subsequent sixteenth note chord with vigor. In m. 67, the progression in the treble should begin a little slowly, get faster on the second beat with an accent on the last eighth-note of the measure, and then slow down again in m. 68, with an accent on the first beat of this measure, and also on the last eighth note octave. In m. 71, the sixteenth-note octave C in the treble, on the first beat of the measure, should be accentuated and the phrase be held back a little on the first quarter of the measure and then proceed quicker towards the end of it. Coming to m. 77, there are accents on the second-half of the first, second, and third beats, on the dotted sixteenth-note chords, while the cadenza scale upwards must be played as the similar one which we have already met with in m. 30. The top B♭ in the treble, on the second beat of m. 80, should be taken with the left hand, as in a similar progression already noted in m. 48.

At m. 81, we arrive at the second part of the Polonaise, which is quite distinct in character and opens with great chords in the key of four sharps, as though the militant spirits, having been aroused and marshaled, in the first part of the Polonaise, were now forming themselves in array for battle. These chords must sound very full and harmonious, like the resounding calls of some beckoning Fate; and they should be deliberate in tempo. Measure 83 introduces a great staccato octave figure which runs through seventeen measures and then repeats itself making thirty-four measures of octaves in all.

Those Fatal Octaves

This figure should commence *pianissimo* and mysteriously, like the galloping of horses in the distance. The octaves, which go on for so long, may become an almost unbearable strain on the left hand, and I find it a relief to think of them technically as proceeding in a semicircular motion from left to right, as in the accompanying diagram, which illustrates the mental device of placing each group of four octaves as component parts of half a circle.

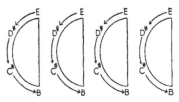

This mechanical illusion of the action of the hands passing in a semicircle over the octaves helps to lessen the tension both mentally of the brain, and physically of the wrist. In m. 88, the three chords in the right hand on the second and third beats should be emphasized. Also the rhythmic figures occurring in m. 89, in the treble, on the second half of the second beat, and on the third beat, should be brought out, together with the same figure arising in the middle voice in m. 91, in the right hand, on the second half of the first beat, and on the second beat. At the end of m. 96, on the last sixteenth-note, the C✕ in the bass and the A♯ in the right hand lead to a very abrupt change of key, which must be strongly marked; as also in m. 99, the two sixteenth-note A♯s, on the second-half of the second beat, and the two following eighth-note chords on the third beat all in the treble, must be stressed.

In m. 100, the reiterated and accented eighth-note chords must be broadened and given weight by a slowing down of tempo, and similarly the quarter-note chords in m. 102, leading to an accent on the first chord in m. 103. From mm. 103–120, the music is a repetition of what has gone before and must be treated in a like manner. At m. 121 a new episode is introduced with a return to the original key of four flats, and this episode should be played a little slower, the melody in the right hand being particularly brought out and sung.

Towards the end of m. 127, the sound should diminish, reaching a *piano* in m. 128, with a ritardando in the second beat of this measure. The D♮ eighth-note, which is the last note in this 128th measure, in both hands, should be held on a little longer than its value. Thus prepare for the next section in m. 129, which must be played rubato and very melodically. Proceeding to m. 132, the rhythmic figures on the first and second beats in this measure should be accelerated, but slow back on the third beat, reaching initial *tempo* again at the beginning of m. 133. The treble B♭ sixteenth-note in the right hand, which is the second note in m. 135, should be held a little, and each of the trills in m. 136 should be slightly accented. In m. 140, the triplet figures in the right hand should be accelerated on the first and second beats, and retarded to tempo again on the third beat.

Arriving at m. 151, the sixteenth-note runs in this measure should be given a mysterious atmosphere, by playing them very softly, smoothly, and legato. In m. 153, the dotted-eighth-note figure, descending by half tones to the sixteenth-notes below, on the second and third beats of the measure, in both hands, should be emphasized; and in m. 154 there must be a ritardando leading to tempo again where the main theme is renewed at m. 155.

From this point on to the end of the piece, the heroic spirit of the music is intensified, and it must be played with the highest enthusiasm. Coming to m. 162, the rhythmical figure here should be played faster on the second beat, and retarded again on the third beat, whilst m. 163 is in tempo. In m. 164 the staccato chord on the first half of the second beat should break off abruptly, and then the dotted sixteenth-note figure on the second half of this beat should be resumed with an accent. There should be a slight ritardando on the third beat of m. 167, and another starting on the second half of m. 170, but returning to tempo on the second beat of beat of m. 171.

The sixteenth-note staccato chords, on the second half of the first beat in m. 172, must be played very rhythmically and an accent be given on the second-half of the second beat in m. 173, on the first sixteenth-note of the triplet arpeggio which begins here. In m. 177, the tempo must accelerate and then slow down again on the second beat of m. 178, whilst the final rhythmical figure in m. 179, on the last two beats of the measure, must be played majestically, with a very full tone, thereby bringing the work to a close of power and decision, befitting the stirring and martial spirit which permeates the whole composition.

POLONAISE
IN A FLAT MAJOR

FR. CHOPIN, Op. 53

A Master Lesson
Dvořák's Slavonic Dance, Op. 72, No. 10
By the World-Renowned Piano Virtuoso
MARK HAMBOURG

[March 1933]

Antonín Dvořák, who was born in 1841 and died in 1904, ranks with his equally distinguished countryman, Smetana, as supreme amongst Czech composers and indeed as one of the most gifted musicians of the nineteenth century. All Dvořák's music bears the imprint not only of his Czech origin but of his typical Slavonic temperament. The great success of his compositions abroad made him therefore feel it an imperative duty both to his art and to his country to emphasize the Czech element in his music and thus obtain recognition for its charm. He greatly admired the national dances which seemed to him peculiarly expressive of his country.

Dvořák wrote two sets of Slavonic dances, the first set, Op. 46, being published in 1878. The collection from which our example here is taken is, however, from the second series, numbered Op. 72. Both these sets of dances first appeared in the form of pianoforte duets, though later Dvořák scored them for orchestra. The dances met with success from the moment they were published.

The Charming Allegretto

Dance No. 10, from the Series Op. 72, being the object of this exposition, is a graceful Allegretto of charm and style. It should be performed with clarity and precision of the rhythmic figures and in a moderate tempo. The staccato accompaniment in the left hand must be negotiated with a stiff wrist and with subdued tone. The first thirty-two measures of the work must be given with reflective feeling, the endeavor being to establish an atmosphere of carefree simplicity. In the fourth measure, the high A staccato sixteenth note written for the left hand can be more easily taken by the right hand. In mm. 9–11, the melody lies in the lower notes of the right hand part and should be brought out, while, in m. 16, the melodic figure is to be found in the bass and must be stressed.

Arriving at m. 24, there should be a diminution of tone towards the end, and the last note C in the left hand should be made prominent. In m. 25, the top notes of the chords in the bass must all be stressed, and a small ritardando made, whereas a kind of portamento effect should be produced when proceeding to D in m. 26, which note should be played by the right hand. The music in this measure should revert to the original tempo. In m. 32 each note in the treble may be slightly accented.

The fingering which I use for the whole piece is written above each note in the printed music as required.

Contrasting Second Movement

The second part of this graceful dance assumes a different character from what has gone before and must be played in a lively, rhythmical manner.

The quick running figures in the left hand in mm. 33–34 must be given significance, the right hand meanwhile being strongly marcato. In juxtaposition to these two measures, the two following ones must be very tender and expressive. It is advisable to take the last two sixteenth notes in the thirty-sixth measure with the right hand instead of the left, as it is written, for this facilitates the execution. Measure 37 should be *piano* in tone, but similar in character to mm. 33 and 34, whilst mm. 39

and 40 must be again played expressively like mm. 35 and 36. Coming to m. 43, the top notes of the broken chords in the bass should be declaimed, and the tone should rise to *forte* in the following measure; but in m. 45 the tone diminishes to *piano*, and in this measure and the next one a reflective character should be reassumed in the interpretation and continued thus until the end of m. 48 where a small pause may be made. The melody is allotted to the left hand from mm. 41–48, and so the left hand should predominate.

The Folk Song Theme

The new theme which commences *a tempo* in mm. 49 and 50 is a real Bohemian folk song and should therefore be interpreted with a singing tone and tense expression.

I make a slight pause on the last chord in m. 50 and a similar pause on the last chord in m. 54; a little ritardando is made in m. 56 and a further pause on the last chord in this measure. The whole music from mm. 49–56 must be played very seriously, with grave dignity. In contrast to this, the same theme played in the higher octave at m. 57 and onward to m. 64 should become slightly humorous, even jaunty.

I do not make a sforzando on the first note of m. 68 in the bass, as is [often] printed there, but, in m. 74, I make a slight pause on the first chord in the right hand, holding back the melody just a little. From mm. 77–84, the tempo should be somewhat slower and the theme which appears in the left hand must be prominent. This theme should be played smoothly, softly, tenderly.

Proceeding to m. 99, it will be found easier to take the chord written for the right hand with the left hand, and the staccato sixteenth notes written in the treble clef for the left hand can then be played with the right hand. In m. 100, the figure in the bass must stand out. As a matter of fact the music from m. 85 onward to the end of the piece is substantially a repetition of what has gone before and must be interpreted in a similar spirit, with the exception of m. 109, where the sixteenth notes marked staccato in the right hand should be emphasized, and in m. 115, where the chord written for the right hand is more easily played by the left hand, as in m. 99. The left-hand staccato notes can then again be played by the right hand. In m. 120, I take the last sixteenth note figure written in the bass part with the right hand.

The Ending on Pianissimo

The piece ends somewhat abruptly, without any kind of peroration, and to make it culminate satisfactorily the tone should sink to *pianissimo* as marked in m. 122. The second and third sixteenth notes, namely G and F♯ in the left hand in m. 123, must sound out with soft insistence, and the two following measures should rise in tone again, leading to *forte* on the chord in m. 126. The sixteenth note figure in the bass in mm. 124 and 125 with its imitation in the treble ought to be very much emphasized, and I personally finish the piece with two *forte* chords in mm. 127 and 128, instead of *pianissimo* as it is marked, because the *forte* gives more finality.

Thus the dance ends simply, a narrative convincingly terminated, without undue flourish or pretension.

SLAVONIC DANCE

ANTONÍN DVOŘÁK
Edited by MARK HAMBOURG

Grieg's "Norwegian Bridal Procession"
A Master Lesson by PERCY GRAINGER
Analyzed and Edited for Study by the Distinguished Australian Composer-Pianist

[November 1920]

Musically speaking, the last half century has been remarkable for the compelling influence exerted by peasant music and primitive music upon great composers in many countries—upon such leaders of musical thought as Grieg, Balakirev, Rimsky-Korsakov, Tchaikovsky, Stravinsky, Brahms, Bartók, Dvořák, Sibelius, Julius Roentgen [1855-1932], Delius, Vaughan Williams, Charles Stanford [1852-1924], Howard Brockway [1870-1951], John Alden Carpenter [1876-1951], Debussy, Ravel, Albéniz, Granados, and many others.

To such an extent have most recent great composers fed upon peasant and popular music and the suggestions and atmosphere emanating therefrom that it is hardly too much to assert that the presence of vital musical geniuses has been increasingly noticeable in countries still possessing a well-preserved peasant culture and that, on the other hand, musical creativity and originality (personal as well as racial) has tended to languish in lands where peasant music is no longer a living art. Nor is this condition of things so surprising when we consider that peasant music is a storehouse of the rural creative life, not of one century but of several, if not innumerable, centuries.

In considering the peasant and primitive music of America and its results we should not forget those two superlatively fine volumes for voice and piano by Howard Brockway: *Lonesome Tunes* and *Kentucky Mountain Tunes*, which should be consulted by everyone interested either in modern music or in archaic song.

Grieg is one of the most striking examples of a great modern creative soul drinking draughts of inspiration at the ancient well of primitive music. Yet a portion only of the strange vitality and weird originality of his musical speech may be ascribed to this source, for the rare flavor of his muse is due primarily to the fact that he combines in great fullness two sides of his art rarely possessed equally by one and the same individual; strong national and local characteristics on the one hand and an unusually highly-developed degree of cosmopolitan musical culture on the other. In this respect he has much in common with Chopin. Both present distinctly national and local characteristics in their work, but they present these characteristics with a creative and technical resourcefulness born of wide experience of diverse schools of composition of various lands and times.

The presentation of national and racial traits alone, interesting though they usually are, would seldom raise the composer's output above being a curiosity. It is the infusion of deep personality and broad erudition into the task of voicing national and racial traits that entitles men such as Grieg, Chopin, Tchaikovsky, Delius and Albéniz to the title of first-class geniuses.

It is the greatest possible mistake to regard Grieg as a "simple" composer in any sense. To the uninitiated, perhaps some of his work may sound simple enough; but to the ears of cultured musicians his music abounds with a unique richness of subtle intricacies. In particular his harmonies are strangely complex, and in this respect stand closer to those of Bach and Wagner than do most modern composers.

In the realm of harmony Grieg was a daring innovator (whose most iconoclastic flights in this direction can most profitably be studied in his amazing arrangements for piano of Norwegian folksongs and dances,

Opus 66 and Opus 72), so much so that it may safely be said that the later moderns of different countries, such as Debussy, MacDowell, Cyril Scott, Delius, John Alden Carpenter, Howard Brockway, Puccini, Albéniz, etc., owe more, harmonically, to the pregnant suggestions of Wagner's and Grieg's harmonic innovations than they do to the influence of any other two composers.

In mm. 56 and 57 of the composition before us we find a rare gem of Grieg's harmonic originality. The eerie "Northern" tang of this chordal shift does not grow stale with time, but is as fresh and as refreshing today as when it first was penned.

Viewing the composition as a whole, however, we must admit that it is the local Norwegian note struck in the *Bridal Procession*, rather than cosmopolitan complexities of workmanship, that constitute its chief characteristics and appeal. Nevertheless, there is here, as always when analyzing Grieg's music, the danger of attributing too much to national traits and too little to the originality and fertility of the composer's purely personal inventive power.

The more we examine Norwegian folk-music the more are we likely to become convinced that a great many of the most salient characteristics of Grieg's music (thoughtlessly dubbed "Norwegian" or "national" by those ignorant of the folksongs of his native land) are, in reality, Griegian and personal and not of racial or popular origin at all.

This point has been ably and repeatedly made by Henry T. Finck [1854-1926], whose book, *Grieg and His Music* [1909], was considered the finest of all the Grieg biographies (in any language) by Grieg himself.

In this connection it is, perhaps, worth remarking that many of the rhythms and melodic lines of the *Bridal Procession* bear quite as close a resemblance to certain Scotch Strathspeys (such as *Tullochgorum*, for instance) as they do to Norwegian dance tunes. Throughout Grieg's music may be found many striking likenesses to certain characteristics of Scottish song, which is the more interesting when we recall that Grieg's parental great-grandfather, Alexander Grieg, was a Scotchman who migrated from Scotland to Norway after the battle of Colloden (1746).

Grieg composed the *Norwegian Bridal Procession* at the age of twenty-six, at an unusually happy period of his life, two years after his marriage to Nina Hagerup, his cousin, and shortly after the birth of their only child, a daughter, whose death, soon to ensue, cast a shadow over the rest of their lives. That Grieg at this juncture was fired with the wish to voice in cultured musical forms the local characteristics of Norway, and of the Norwegian peasants in particular, is borne out in the following excerpt of a letter recently written to me by Madame Nina Grieg, the widow of the composer, and here translated from the Norwegian of the original:

" 'The Bridal Procession Passes By' was written in 1889 at 'Landaas,' Grieg's childhood home near Bergen (Norway). Landaas was a lovely property, close under 'Ulrikken,' one of Bergen's seven mountains. It had belonged to Governor (Stiftamtmand) Hagerup, who was Grieg's grandfather as well as mine, and he had presented it to Grieg's mother. She had prepared in the 'stabur' (rural storehouse) a musical workroom with a piano in it for her beloved son, and here it was that he composed, in addition to the 'Bridal Procession,' songs such as 'The First Meeting,' 'Good Morning,' 'Woodland Wandering' and many others. He worked there with such joy and freshness when we first arrived, but later was stricken with the sorrow of the death of our little daughter, and, as far as I remember, never composed there again.

Grieg was, as you know, Norwegian through and through, and at that period of his life was highly enthusiastic about the Norwegian peasants and all that pertained to them. Later on this enthusiasm lessened, yet the strong influence of his native land and its local color never left him—fortunately."

Though Grieg, later in life, experienced the disillusionment with regard to the Norwegian peasants alluded to in the above letter, yet as a musician he ever remained their loyal interpreter, as is evident in the piano volumes, Opus 66 and Opus 72, already alluded to, no less than in his incomparable songs to poems written in the peasant tongue by the poets Vinje, Arne Garborg and others, such as *On the Journey Home, The Wounded Heart* and the exquisite cycle, *The Mountain Maid* ("Haugtussa").

The title *Norwegian Bridal Procession Passes By* was frequently used by Grieg for this piece, and it, more clearly than the more familiar title *Norwegian Bridal Procession*, reveals the exact nature of the effect to be striven for in rendering it; the impression of a peasant bridal march, played at the head of a bridal procession on its way to church for the wedding ceremony, first heard faintly from afar (mm. 1–24), then gradually drawing nearer (mm. 25–67), passing the listener close by in a turmoil of clamor and color (mm. 68–101), and finally gradually becoming distant once more until at last its strains are well nigh inaudible (mm. 102–129).

Throughout the composition the clanging of church bells is heard blended with the sounds of the bridal march music. This is particularly manifest in the section embracing mm. 80–93, while it is not improbable that the introduction (mm. 1–4) and the repetitions of this section throughout, were likewise intended by Grieg to portray a suggestion of distant church chimes.

Throughout the section beginning at m. 25 the pianist should strive to imitate, in the persistent rhythms of the left hand, the monotonous "sawing" of the peasant fiddler.

In order to convey the impression of the wedding party proceeding to the church to the strains of peasant march music, the pianist should play the piece in metronomically strict time throughout. Any momentary or more protracted alteration of speed in such a composition can only act as a blemish and as a frustration of the obvious intention of the composer. The work should be conceived and rendered *as march music* from first to last; as a solemn, sturdy, *processional* march, with the feet of the marching bridal party falling upon the quarter-notes, twice in every measure.

Most students will derive much benefit from practicing mainly with the metronome, oftenest at slow speed (say M. M. 108 to the eighth-notes) and sometimes, but less often, with the metronome at the full speed indicated in my edition.

Every effort should be made to make the impression of distance, gradual approach, closeness, gradual passing by, distance as vivid and sensational as possible and to this end the pianist should not scruple to employ an exaggerated degree of *pianissimo* at the opening and at the close of the composition, and should strive to work up to a clanging riotous *fortissimo* at the climax (mm. 68–101).

Pianists in general are too chary of utilizing the extremes of *pianissimo* of which the piano is capable. With practice, the very softest tones can be controlled almost as easily as louder sounds, the more so if the student will avoid attacking *pp* and *ppp* notes too close to the keys. We should remember that the piano is more naturally adapted to the production of extremely soft sounds than most other instruments, as its very softest tones do not deteriorate in quality of tone or in pitch as equally soft tones are apt to do with most wind and string instruments. The only danger, in attempting to produce an extreme *pp* upon the piano, is that some of the notes may not sound at all. Students must not be afraid to "take a chance" in such cases, for an occasional silent note is preferable to the failure to attain an extreme *pianissimo*, particularly in a dynamically sensational composition such as the *Norwegian Bridal Procession*.

Hints for Study

The students attention is especially called to two salient points of modern pianism: (1) the sustaining pedal, (2) non-stretch fingering.

The growing realization of the advantages to be derived from the liberal use of the sustaining (or "sostenuto" or "middle") pedal has, during recent years, developed, extended and perfected piano playing more than any other single factor; so much so that in the near future a pianist not availing himself of the advantages of this truly wonderful American invention will be as much out of date as the dodo—as much of an anachronism as is today a pianist making no use of the damper pedal.

Students, in buying a piano or selecting one for practice, should be careful to see that the instrument is equipped with sustaining pedal action throughout the entire length of the damper system (about 5 1/2 octaves, beginning with the lowest note of the instrument), and should make sure that the sustaining pedal functions correctly.

A properly functioning sustaining pedal will, as long as it is pressed down, clearly sustain any note or notes (within the aforesaid damper system), the keys of which were pressed down prior to the depressing of the sustaining pedal, and *will not* (as will the damper pedal) sustain any note or notes played *after* the depression of the sustaining pedal, provided the following three rules are faithfully carried out:

(1) The note or notes to be sustained by the sustaining pedal must be pressed down *before* the sustaining pedal is depressed, otherwise the sustaining pedal will not take effect upon that note or notes.

(2) The note or notes to be sustained by the sustaining pedal must be held down by the fingers until the sustaining pedal is *fully depressed*, otherwise the sustaining pedal will not take effect upon that note or notes.

(3) The damper pedal must *always* be *fully raised* at the moment of pressing down the sustaining pedal, otherwise the sustaining pedal, as long as it is held down, will "sustain" the entire damper system and a complete blur will result, thus defeating the whole object of the sustaining pedal. Immediately the sustaining pedal is *fully depressed*, however, and at any time during its retention, the damper pedal may be freely used and delightful new effects produced by the cooperation of these two pedals.

The object of a lavish use of the sustaining pedal is the attainment of greater tonal clarity, and the result of this clarification is a strong influence in the direction of greater refinement and subtlety of performance, purging the student's playing of "banging" no less than of "blurring," if rightly understood and applied.

Enlightened pianists employ the sustaining pedal almost as extensively as they do the damper pedal, and I would strongly advise all pianists hitherto unfamiliar with its technic to acquire the "sustaining pedal habit" as soon as possible, to which end the indications of sustaining pedaling in this edition may serve as a modest beginning.

In order to attain reliability of performance we should avoid, as far as possible, all fingerings that demand big stretches of the hand. The more we indulge in stretched positions, the more numb and cramped the hand feels, the less conscious of its exact space-relation to the keys about to be played, and, consequently, the poorer our control and mastery of the passage in hand. Therefore the experienced pianist substitutes *frequent small groupings* or divisions of fingering for *less frequent larger groupings* or divisions of fingering, wherever feasible. For instance, extended chords, such as:

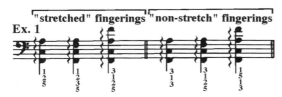

can be played with *greater reliability* with the fingerings marked "non-stretch" [during figurations that are linearized] than with the fingerings marked "stretched," once we have somewhat familiarized ourselves with the non-stretch system.

The student will find numerous instances of the non-stretch modern method of fingering if he will [study] my fingerings in the present edition, notably in the following measures: 41 (right hand), 63, 64, 79–80 (broken chord in left hand), 80 (right hand), 83–84 (broken chord in left hand), 84 (right hand), 94, 95, 98, 99, 111, 115.

Grainger Edition
Considered in Detail for Keyboard Practice

Measure 1. Play the two bass notes E, B, *before* taking the sustaining pedal with the left foot and be sure to hold these notes down with the fingers until the sustaining pedal has *really taken effect* upon them. Take care not to press down the damper pedal while pressing down the sustaining pedal.

In the following measures (2–24, inclusive) the bass notes E, B, on the first beat of each measure, should be played extra soft, being sustained as they are in the sustaining pedal, and therefore likely to "boom" on objectionably if inadvertently struck too loudly. The relative dynamic values obtaining in m. 1, and wherever this figure occurs are indicated:

Measure 2. See that the damper pedal is raised *together* with the striking of the eighth-note chord G♯, E in the right hand, so that the staccato nature of this chord is fully realized. Note that throughout the entire composition, wherever this rhythmic chordal figure occurs (mm. 1–2, 4–11, 13–14, 16–23, 96–97–100–101, 104–105–108–109, 112–113, 116–125, 127) my damper pedaling is planned to permit the second eighth-note of the measure to be sounded staccato. The hands must cooperate with the damper pedal in producing this staccato effect, and care should be taken to maintain, throughout, relative dynamic values similar to those indicated in Example 2. Thus, in m. 96 the actual dynamic values should be as shown:

Measure 5. Be careful to subdue the tone of the left hand so that the listener's chief attention may be directed to the melody of the right hand. Almost all students, and many mature pianists as well, play their accompaniments too loud for their melodies and forget, in particular, how *much louder* high treble notes need to be played in order to make them ring out prominently above the far greater natural sonority of low bass notes. The same precaution should be taken with all similar passages, such as those beginning at mm. 25, 56, 70, 110.

Measure 5. Be scrupulous to preserve the exact rhythmic relationship between the dotted sixteenth-notes and the thirty-second notes, Too often this passage is played with the sound of triplets:

This tendency can be corrected by practicing the passage as indicated:

Count four to every eighth-note, and be sure that the thirty-second-notes are not played before "four" is counted. Inexperienced musicians are apt to cut the duration of the dotted notes *too short* in cases such as these. This error can also be corrected by practicing the passage with a metronome ticking four times in each measure, and playing the thirty-second notes like very quick grace notes:

Measure 6. The accent on the G♯ of the right hand seen in the original (Grieg) edition is probably an error, as no similar accent occurs on the corresponding notes in mm. 5, 9 and 10.

Measure 13. The soft pedal (una corda) has to be taken by the left foot *without releasing the sustaining pedal* (likewise negotiated by the left foot). In order to accomplish this the sustaining pedal should be held down *by the tip* of the left shoe, while the heel is raised upwards and outward (the left knee turning inward towards the right knee) until the ball of the left foot is able to rise above the soft pedal and press it down. When both the soft and the sustaining pedals are thus held down by the left foot the position of that foot will be nearly at right angles to the position of the right foot (which retains its usual position), with the toes of the left foot turned in towards the right foot and the heel turned outwards towards the bass end of the piano. Though this position seems very awkward at first, it can readily be acquired and effortlessly controlled with a few weeks practice. This branch of technic should not be neglected by the student, since the simultaneous use of the soft and the sustaining pedals by the left foot is a constant necessity in modern music and an indispensable adjunct to mature pianism.

Measures 13–24 should sound like a kind of echo of mm. 1–12, and should, therefore be played just as softly as possible.

Measure 25. What was remarked regarding the rhythm of m. 5 applies with particular force to the continuous figure of dotted sixteenth-notes and thirty-second-notes that are found throughout the following measures: 25–59, 62–72, 74–76, 78, 80–89. Take care not to let this degenerate into the triplet rhythm shown in Example 7.

In order to guard against this tendency think of each thirty-second-note as belonging to the *following* (not to the *preceding*) dotted sixteenth-note, and practice the passage along the lines indicated in Ex. 5 and 6.

Measure 26. Before taking the sustaining pedal at the beginning of this measure be sure that the damper pedal (held down until the end of the preceding measure) is *fully raised*. The same care should be exercised at mm. 28, 34, 36, etc., wherever the sustaining pedal follows immediately after the use of the damper pedal.

Measures 49–50–51. Play the thirty-second-note in the left hand *well after* the third note of the right hand triplet. In particular avoid the slovenly performance of m. 51 shown in Example 8.

Measures 54, 55. "Half-pedaling" means *partially* raising the damper pedal, so that the dampers *only partially* damp the vibrations of the strings—not wholly, as is the case when the damper pedal is completely raised. By half-pedaling at m. 54 we cut off part of the large volume of sound that has been accumulating in the damper pedal since the beginning of m. 52. By half pedaling again at m. 55 we still further reduce this resonance. The result of such half-pedaling, if correctly carried out, produces a kind of echo-sensation.

Measures 69–71. Here is a typical use of the sustaining pedal. The bass notes E, B, E, B, secured by the sustaining pedal on the second beat of m. 69 (be sure you hold these notes down with the fingers until the sustaining pedal has taken effect upon them) are thus safely sustained until the beginning of m. 72, while the damper pedal is used to add a short gush of resonance to the four accented notes in each measure. This is an instance of the clarifying effect of the sustaining pedal. Without it we would have to swamp the greater part of the passage in a damper pedal blur in order to retain the drone effect of the bass notes E, B (so obviously intended to he heard ringing on until the end of m. 71), or we would have to forego the drone effect, at least partially, in the interests of tonal cleanliness. By using the sustaining pedal and the damper pedal in conjunction we are able to combine complete clarity with a fully carried out drone effect.

Measures 70, 71, 74, 75. Use either the fingering above or the fingering below the notes of the left hand. The upper fingering is the more powerful vehicle. It is carried out as follows: In the case of white keys the tips of the first, second and third fingers are held tightly bunched together, the key being struck by the third finger. In the case of black keys, the fourth finger is added to the other three, all four are held tightly bunched together, and the key is struck by the fourth finger. This method of fingering, so widely used concert pianists in martellato passages, can be practiced in both hands as shown in Example 9.

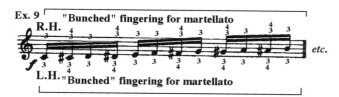

Measure 73. The sustaining pedal should not be pressed down until the right hand has been raised at the sixteenth note rest. Care should be taken that the bass notes E, B, E in the left hand are held down by the fingers (*after* the right hand has been raised) until the sustaining pedal has taken effect upon them. The same applies to the use of the damper

pedal in mm. 77 and 79.

Measure 79. Be sure the last two notes of this measure (C♯ and A♯ in the left hand) are sounded loudly and held down until the sustaining pedal has been fully depressed. The whole effect of the ensuing section (mm. 80–83) demands a very resonant retention of these bass notes C♯, A♯ in the sustaining pedal. The same vigor and care should he exercised in establishing and securing in the sustaining pedal the bass notes B, A occurring at the end of m. 83, for similar reasons.

Measure 80. Here, for the first time in the composition, the melody is in the left hand, and that hand should be played very considerably louder than the right hand throughout the whole of this section (mm. 80–89). Indeed, the left hand should play with great roughness—but with a *controlled* roughness, of course; emphasizing the accented notes well above the rest. The remarks about "bunched" fingering attached to m. 70 apply here with equal force.

Measures 90–93. In attacking these *fortissimo* chords the inner fingers (2d, 3d and 4th fingers) of both hands should be used quite as forcibly as the outer fingers (1st and 5th fingers). In most cases the failure to sound the middle notes of loud chords as strongly as the outer notes is due to not advancing the inner fingers (entrusted with the inner notes) far enough *forward* (towards the keys) in relation to the position of the outer fingers, or to the inability of the player to hold the fingers rigid at the moment of striking the keys.

Measure 92. In this case "sostenuto" means "slower."

Measure 94. Distinguish clearly, rhythmically, between the dotted sixteenth-notes and thirty-second-notes on the one hand and the triplets on the other. Do not let it sound as shown in Example 10.

Hold the dotted notes for their full duration and make the thirty-second-notes as short as possible. The same holds good with regard to mm. 95, 98, 99, 102, 103, 106, 107.

Measures 96, 97, 100, 101. The proper dynamic treatment has already been shown in Example 3. The second eighth note in all these measures should be played as short as possible *without, however, playing the next chord (the accented quarter-note) in the very least before its time*. It is a common error, with many players, to cut short the beat value of staccato notes. This is the more unfortunate (apart from the matter of destroying rhythmic accuracy) in that the staccato impression of a note is enhanced by a long, rather than a short, silence between it and the succeeding note.

Measures 104, 105, 108, 109, etc., should dynamically resemble measures 96, 97, 100, 101, but on a smaller, and increasingly diminishing, dynamic scale.

Measure 110. As the music gets softer and softer, from m. 110 to the end of the piece, care should be taken to preserve the dynamic contrasts (between accented and unaccented notes) and durative contrasts (between staccato notes and sustained notes) with due sharpness and vividness. The peasant bridal march music, played at the head of the bridal procession, is not supposed to be being played with decreased vigor. It is merely supposed to be heard by the listener from an ever greater and greater distance, and the performance of the music should, therefore, retain its rhythmic and dynamic physiognomy up to the very last chord.

Dedicated to J. P. E. Hartman

NORWEGIAN BRIDAL PROCESSION

Also published by Grieg with the following title:
"NORWEGIAN BRIDAL PROCESSION PASSES BY"

Nº 2 from "SKETCHES OF NORWEGIAN LIFE"

EDVARD GRIEG, Op. 19, Nº 2

As edited by
Percy Grainger
for study and
concert
performance

Alla Marcia M.M. ♩= about 152

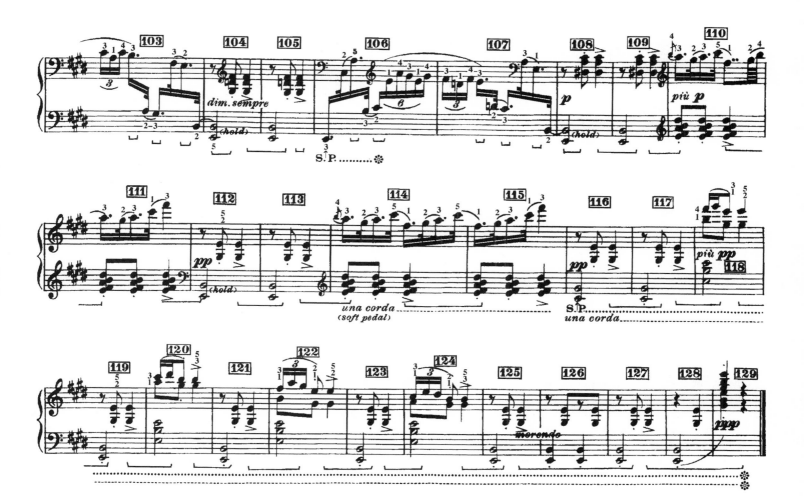

A Master Lesson on the "Liebestraum" of Liszt Prefaced by a Short Note About the Composer

Especially Written for THE ETUDE by the Distinguished Russian Virtuoso

MARK HAMBOURG

[April 1926]

Franz Liszt was born at Raiding in Hungary, on October 22nd, 1811. In versatility he rivals the great artists of the Renaissance. As a pianist he was supreme, and his concert tours were so many triumphal progresses throughout Europe. Under his leadership the orchestra at Weimar became one of the finest, and Weimar itself the centre of German artistic musical life. Many of the greatest pianists were pupils of Liszt and bear witness to his inspiration as a master.

Success accompanied all he undertook in life, and his compositions for the orchestra, the pianoforte and the voice place him in the forefront of distinguished composers. His literary works, including his articles on Chopin and those on the music of the Gypsies, written in German and in French, reveal the fact that he had a remarkable command over style and language. He holds a unique position in the history of musical development and is an outstanding figure of the artistic world of his day.

Some of Liszt's most delightful music was inspired by the literature of his day. The French Romantic School with which he became associated during his stay in Paris influenced many of the compositions in his "Années de Pélérinage"; but this *Liebestraum* was inspired by a poem by Freiligrath, and it is a good example of the "Salon" music of which Liszt was such a master. It is published in a series of three Nocturnes entitled *Dreams of Love*, and is one of the most popular of the composers works. He has embellished his theme with consummate art, and no one who has heard the *Liebestraum* can fail to appreciate its charm. Graceful and entrancing melody is combined in it with a certain dignity and depth of feeling, and ornamented with delicate and brilliant arabesques. Above the opening measures is printed a sonnet by F[erdinand] Freiligrath [1810-1876]. It exhorts the lover to love always with the utmost of his being, while he may, and never to let a harsh word escape him, as death so soon brings separation and regrets.

In this atmosphere of intense feeling tinged with melancholy the melody of the nocturne should open.

The Melody Sings

The song must be brought out in declamatory style, as if sung by a singer with all the correct relief and elasticity of rhythm for taking in breath at the right moments. The arpeggio-like accompaniment in the right hand should be played throughout with a juicy tone, not only as a mere figure but as a sensuous adjunct to the melody. In m. 5 the notes F, G, A♭, C, B♭ in the left hand, and A♭ in the succeeding measure, must be especially emphasized and played rubato to give stress of feeling to the end of the phrase.

In m. 8, on the fourth beat in the bass there is a G♭ which should be brought out. In m. 10 on the high F in the left hand, a pause can be made amounting almost to a fermata.

In m. 11, as before in m. 5, the phrase F, G, A♭, C, B♭, A♭ should be declaimed in rubato fashion, with a rise in tone on the culminating C and then a drop back to the A♭ in the twelfth measure. In m. 16 there should be a crescendo beginning on the first E♮ on the first beat, and proceeding to the second E♮ in the middle part, but dropping immediately to *piano* again on the first beat of the seventeenth measure. At m. 21 a spirit of agitation should be introduced, the tempo being slightly quickened, and a crescendo rising from the emphasized B♭ of the melody on the first beat of the measure to the D♭ half-note on the fourth beat. From this fourth beat to the C♭ on the sixth beat of this same measure the tone should decrease and then rise again in m. 22 to the F♭ on the fourth beat, slowing down with emphasis on the notes A♭ and B♭ on the fifth and sixth beats in the bass of the measure. The culmination of the agitation is reached on the F♭ fermata in the twenty-third measure and then descends in a declamatory phrase to G♮ on the first beat of the twenty-fourth measure, which should also be held like a fermata. A long pause must be made before attacking the ensuing cadenza. This should start *piano* and not very fast, and then crescendo and accelerando with four well-marked accents on the first, second, third and fourth double notes of the figure in the right hand on the third beat of the twenty-fifth measure. The rest of the figure should be made to sound like a rippling cascade of water falling down in a silver shower and getting slower and slower at the end as the rush dies away. Four accents should be given on the first four notes of the double tremolo which terminates the cadenza, and the tremolo should be kept on and repeated as many times as the technic of the performer permits.

Taking Breath

A long pause must then be made, as if to take breath, and then the main theme appears in the right hand (this time in B major). The music is here marked *Più animato, con passione*; but I do not play it so, but start the song at this point quite quietly and dreamily. In the twenty-ninth measure the tone should sink somewhat from the accented D♯ on the first beat of the measure to the G♯ on the fourth beat. The first, second and third quarter-notes in the treble in m. 30 should be emphasized and the whole phrase declaimed, whilst the second figure in the bass in m. 31 must be brought out with a welling crescendo and decrescendo. I play m. 32 a little slower and m. 33 a little faster, and m. 35 again slower, to create variation of expression; and I bring out the accompaniment very much in both hands. In m. 36 the declamatory passage in octaves should be played very rubato, leading up to a big pause and fermata on the fourth beat of the same measure.

The thirty-seventh measure should be resumed *a tempo* in the key of C major. The passage in the accompaniment in this measure is made easier by taking the first four notes of it with the right hand with fingers 5–2–3–1, and then continuing the rest of the passage with the left hand. An accent may be given to the chord on the first beat of m. 39 and the melody should begin to rise in an atmosphere of gathering emotion up to the *fortissimo* in m. 41, where everything should sound marcato and dramatic, and should continue in suppressed excitement. In m. 44, I give an emphasis on the note G♯ on the fourth beat, at the beginning of the descending figure in the left hand, and also emphasis on the chords on the first, second and third beats in the right hand in the forty-fifth measure.

From mm. 47–50 the tempo should be quickened, and then broadened out again in the fiftieth measure. A decrescendo to the middle of that measure, rising once more in crescendo to the chord on the first beat of m. 51 is very effective. In m. 52 there are octaves in triplets in the right hand, each note of which must be emphasized; and again in m. 54 the triplet passages in the treble must be declaimed and lead up to a big pause on the octave G. Proceeding after the pause, the next passage in the fifty-fifth measure must be played very rubato, with a decrescendo to the middle of the measure, and then a crescendo with prominence given to the octaves G and A♭. These octaves lead on to an accelerando of tempo in the next two measures, and to a big attack of the chord on the first beat of m. 58, where the final cadenza breaks away.

The top note of the cadenza on F♮ in the right hand should receive an accent; and then the tone should diminish as the big passage descends the first time. It should rise again with quickening of speed and accents on each of the E♭s at the beginning of the three ascending *arpeggi*, culminating in a *fortissimo* on C, D♭, A♮, B♭, F♯ and G, which are the first six notes of the final descending passage, and should be played slightly slower with accents. From these six notes onwards the cadenza should descend faster and faster like a ball bouncing down hill from one stone to another, until it slows up with a slight crescendo and then a decrescendo in the last seventeen notes of the passage.

Return of First Theme

After a pause, the original melody is now resumed and should start with a lingering attack from the upbeat on E♭ to the C on the first beat of m. 61, holding the C on just a trifle longer than its real value. This part of the *Liebestraum* must be played reflectively and tenderly, endeavoring to give an effect as of a remembrance of the opening measures of the piece. The tone produced ought to be what I call *flebile*, meaning by that an intangible, faraway sound. The notes on the first, second, third and fourth beats of m. 65 should be brought out with feeling, and the accompaniment in m. 66 should have an atmosphere of intensity with a rising and falling of tone.

The tempo should be somewhat broadened in m. 69, with a lingering attack again from the C on the last beat in the treble of that measure to the long F in the next measure. From here on I introduce some fluctuation of tempo. [In] m. 71 I play somewhat slower; m. 72 is in tempo again; m. 73 is lingering; m. 74 in tempo; and then from m. 75 onwards there should be a gradual and continuous slackening of speed, the fingers trailing on the notes as if loath to leave them. The whole of m. 76 must be very much retarded, and each of the last four notes in it emphasized, whilst m. 77 should be performed as if the notes were almost being spoken "*recitativo*," rather than played, and trying to give an effect as of a question asked. A long pause in measure eighty brings us to the final chords of the piece, which are marked in the music **mp**. But I start these chords in *mezzo forte* with a good large tone, and then make a gradual decrescendo, pressing out the notes of the melody in the middle parts in mm. 83–84: namely, C, B♮; C, E♭; D♭, C; with a final fervor of expiring emotion.

Too much Reserve
Mark Hambourg
[November 1924]

Young students often come to play to me who are already far advanced in technical facility. They play me a difficult piece with perfect accuracy, fluency, and show a high level of proficiency; yet the whole performance is so dull and lifeless that I can scarcely bear to sit it out to the end. What is it that is lacking? Well, there are various subtle qualities to be acquired in piano playing before it can become interesting, even though the player be a very good performer in the ordinary sense of the word. That is to say, he plays all the notes and makes few mistakes. But if he does not succeed in giving pleasure to his hearers, what is the use of all his proficiency?

Something which affects piano playing can be laid to the charge of the education at present so in vogue, which teaches self-repression as one of the cardinal virtues and that emotion should be hidden away as much as possible rather than be expressed. The reserve thus built up by the general spirit of such education is hard to break down and often holds in a vise the temperament of people who would fain express themselves but cannot "out with it." I remember when I was a small boy studying with Leschetizsky, that in the class one day while one of the pupils was playing, the Professor suddenly lit a candle and put it under the chair the boy was sitting on. "To warm his playing up a bit," he explained to us.

It is a curious thing that many people possess in themselves a very great deal of temperament and yet cannot communicate any of its warmth to their audience by their performance of music. They cannot get it across the footlights, as the actors call it. This renders their playing unconvincing, and they are unable to really carry away their hearers; in fact (and now we have arrived at the crux of the whole matter) they lack Personality. Personality, that mysterious something which is everything; power, imagination, temperament, charm, all are contained and ruled by that strange intangible force which no one can explain. I doubt whether it can be acquired. It is a gift which Nature either bestows or withholds. Therefore, in my opinion, the best teachers are those who endeavor to develop personality wherever they spy it in their pupils, not those who try to impose their own ego, and stifle the budding soul of the neophyte, telling him that only technical accuracy is of importance. Many young people only need sympathetic stimulus to find out how to express themselves, and if they are taught on the piano the several means which they can use to help to that end they can have no excuse afterwards for their playing being dull and uninteresting. Then the reason must be that from their own natures they have nothing to give out. For, primarily, if the artist is to be interesting at all, he must himself have some esthetic message to bring, even when he is only a reproducing artist as is the pianist. The thought, light, and imagination that the performer is able to throw into the music he has set out to play, make it constantly re-live and recapture the attention of his audience. The end of it all is that no matter how skillfully a pianist plays the notes which are written, unless he can put into his music variety of touch, pulse of rhythm, contrasts of light and shade in the quality of his sound, his playing will remain dull and monotonous to listen to and will never uplift his hearers into the highest artistic communion with himself.

Love Dreams
No. 3

Poem by Freiligrath

Oh! love while love is left to thee;
  Oh! love while love is yet thine own;
The hour will come when bitterly
  Thou'lt mourn by silent graves, alone!

And let thy breast with kindness glow,
  And gentle thoughts within thee move,
While yet a heart, through weal and woe,
  Beats to thine own in faithful love.

And who to thee his heart doth bare,
  Take heed thou fondly cherish him;
And gladden thou his every hour,
  And not an hour with sorrow dim!

And guard thy lips and keep them still;
  Too soon escapes an angry word:
"Oh God! I did not mean it ill!"
  But yet he sorrowed as he heard.

Poco Allegro, con affetto

Franz Liszt

Arpeggi to be played with juicy tone, not only as a mere accompaniment.

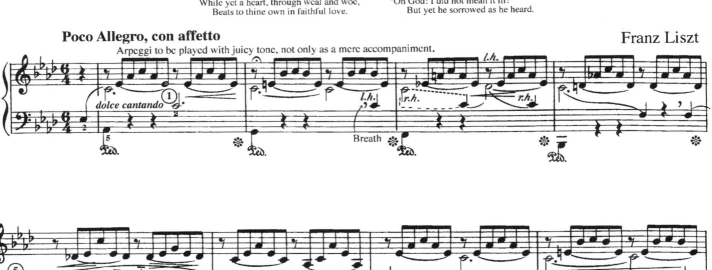

To be played like a remembrance
of the opening bars of the piece.

Tenderly and reflectively.

With good large tone, then *diminuendo,* bringing out well the
notes of melody in the middle parts.

An Analysis Lesson on Edward MacDowell's Witches' Dance

Prepared in Collaboration With

MRS. EDWARD MACDOWELL

[December 1922]

The following lesson upon the *Witches' Dance* by the great American composer, Edward MacDowell, was prepared in collaboration with Mrs. MacDowell, who has hesitated to write definite notes in person. However, all the material is based upon her own suggestions. In many ways the writer feels that it will present new and very different ideas upon the nature and interpretation of this work, one of the most unusual successes in the history of American music.

Edward Alexander MacDowell was born in New York, December 18, 1860. He died there January 23, 1908 and was buried at Peterborough, New Hampshire, where many of his greatest works were created and where has been established The MacDowell Colony to provide for workers in all the creative arts the best working conditions. Already, notable results have been given to the world. MacDowell stands easily at the head of American composers, because of his innate musical gifts, his grasp of musical forms large and small, his facility and logical means of expression and his rich, poetic soul. His muse is, at times, as bold as the mountain tempests, and again as delicate as spring zephyrs in the waving iris.

In publishing the following lesson on the *Witches' Dance* the main body of the text follows pedagogical suggestions made by Mrs. MacDowell.

A Lesson on the *Witches' Dance*

While printed lessons upon a pianoforte composition must, at best, be wholly analytical (there being no opportunity for the teacher's criticism), much can nevertheless be said which will help the active-minded student, who may not have the advantage of a carefully trained instructor.

Behind every composition there is always a background which, when understood, contributes much to the proper interpretation of the composition. Innumerable people essay to play this composition without the slightest idea of what Mr. MacDowell had in mind when he wrote the work. Indeed, many have a totally different conception of the piece from that intended by the composer.

The first error that most people make about the *Witches' Dance* is that they have a different kind of witch in mind. They think of some old hag, like the witches in Macbeth, or, the witches which the good folk of Salem feared when they nightly barred their doors to keep them out. That is not at all the kind of sprite which Mr. MacDowell pictured. It was rather the mischievous demons or elves who fly in clouds through the air, like pixies. They were light gossamery nothings, mischievous, but delicate as a feather, wafted by the swift March breezes. They soured the milk and put a blight upon the wheat, and did all sorts of antics which got people into trouble, but there was nothing heavy or loathsome about them. Because so many people have pictured a malignant old hag, or crone, in association with the *Witches' Dance*, the average student bangs away at the piece and tries to add a kind of tragic or morbid element to it. Mr. MacDowell never had any such thought. He played most of the work as though it were made of thread lace.

[Regarding] the following suggestions given; I am following the precedents set down by him, and in this way I have felt at liberty to do away with one repetition and also to eliminate one extremely awkward passage, which makes the whole work needlessly difficult for many students, and has doubtless placed it beyond the grasp of many who would otherwise be able to play it with pleasure. These changes in no way injure the artistic value of the work. Indeed they are the very changes sanctioned by Mr. MacDowell and often played by him.

The Lesson Begins

Well, let us begin with the lesson. The metronome makes 126 equal a dotted quarter note, a fair speed, but unless you have a remarkable technique, you will find it desirable to begin the study very much slower, possibly, counting at first three beats to the measure, with the eighth note equaling, let us say, 72 or 84. Most teachers find there is an advantage in studying any piece that is to go very fast ultimately, at an aggravatingly slow pace at first. Indeed, it is impossible to study this at first with a high finger action, although when it is really played, the notes trip off in groups from fingers held almost as light as cobwebs.

Imagine at the start that the air is fairly filled with clouds and clouds of pixies, whirling and posing and playing about, bent upon mischief. Catch this spirit from the start. Most of the editions of this work are quite without pedaling, but Mr. MacDowell certainly never played it without using the pedals. In this edition I have endeavored to indicate the pedaling, and this contributes to the gossamer effects of the piece quite as much as anything that can be done with the hands.

In the first measure, at **A**, I would like to call attention to the fact that Mr. MacDowell practically always played the passage so that the grace note in the left hand came first, and not with the first note in the right hand, as it is ordinarily played. In other words, he played the grace note as though it were a part of an imaginary preceding measure, making the first chord as arpeggio, thus—

When the performer has a fine grand piano, it is desirable to use the middle pedal to sustain the bass chord for the first four measures. If you have not such a pedal, employ the regular damper pedal here, because that chord must be heard delicately sustained.

Throughout the composition some students will wonder why the pedal is employed, although the bass notes are marked distinctly staccato. How can a sound be sustained and be staccato? The pedaling in these, played atmospherically, is quite necessary; and if the staccato notes are struck lightly enough, their percussive value will give the suggestion of staccato.

At **B** the cloudy-like flight of the witches really begins. Here the melodic line surges up and down, and the dynamic effects for the most part follow the line. That is, as the melody ascends the melody becomes ever so slightly louder, and as it descends, slightly softer. The hands, after much practice, become very sensitive to these swirls of tone. It must not be played like a Czerny exercise with angular corners.

Little further comment is required until letter **C** is reached. Here the wrist staccato should be as light as possible. Indeed, the effect described by Dr. [William] Mason [1829-1908], in which the hand seems to be lifted sharply from the keys rather than struck, seems to be desirable.

In the interlocking passage at **D**, endeavor to have the right hand and left hand as even as possible. The same is true at **E** and at **F**. Here again the lightness is produced by the illusion of playing as though lifting the hands away from the keys instead of striking them.

The Pedal and Staccato

At **G** do not be afraid of the quick pedal indicated on the bass notes. These are marked staccato, to be true, but Mr. MacDowell always played them with the pedal to avoid a "bony" tone. It is almost impossible to play them in these low registers without giving a too brittle, too thumpy effect.

At **H** begins a kind of triumphant little march as though the pixies were gloating over the accomplishment of their work. Watch the crescendos and the decrescendos here very carefully.

At **I** make the effect with the right hand as much like a trill as possible. Indeed, for these four measures the *tempo* may be slightly accelerated, gradually. All the left-hand notes in these four measures may be made more *staccato* and more dramatic if played with one finger, the second or third finger. In the next four measures, if Mr. MacDowell had a pupil with a small hand, he encouraged him to play the bass thus—

instead of as written.

Indeed, he would often play it this way himself and thought that it added color.

At **J**, a passage which seems to bother some pupils, the difficulty will disappear if it is regarded as being written in 3/4 measure, without the intervening bar line. This applies to all the measures as far as **K**.

At **K** the pixies have worked up to a fine frenzy of impish iniquity; and the one measure rest comes like a flash of silence. The effect is very dramatic if the rest is not overheld. The attention of the audience is smitten by this rest more than it would be by a crashing chord; if the crescendo approaching it is carefully developed and the total silence come abruptly enough.

The theme is resumed again at **L** with thistledown lightness, proceeds to a *fortissimo* at **M**, followed by martellato octaves, which should be judiciously retarded as they approach the entrance of the little march theme. Again at **N** this theme should be played very delicately and sweetly, but not mincingly or with sentimentality. Note the crescendo*s* at **O** and at **P** leading to sfzorandos, and the still greater crescendo at **Q** leading to the climax of the composition at **S**.

A Quick Ending

Again the pixies commence to swarm in the summer night. Dawn is approaching and, like all good pixies, they must soon vanish. Strive for this hushed effect from here to the end. Students familiar with previous editions will find that twenty-four measures here are eliminated which do not add any particular value to the work [at **X**]. Indeed, my impression is that by proceeding to a quick ending the artistic effect is enhanced.

At **T** do not hurry the recitative nor make the frequent mistake of playing it heavily. Remember, these are not the witches of Macbeth. With the prestissimo at **U**, the first shafts of sunlight scatter the whole horde of pixies until they vanish in thin air. The grace notes in measure **U**, as in measure **V**, always precede the bass note and are not played with it.

Note the quick pedal in the last three measures and also the final low B at **W**. This I find myself putting in instinctively, as did Mr. MacDowell, although it appears in none of the editions.

Again let me enjoin the reader to observe the continuity of the melodic line. Mr. MacDowell made melody one of the tenets of his musical creed. If you would play any of the MacDowell compositions, as the composer would have you play them, learn to appreciate first of all the eloquence of their melodies.

[from] **Notes on Modern American Music**
By Walter Spry
[February 1906]

In presenting the subject of modern American music, I am aware that there is a difference of opinion among musicians as to whether such a thing as American music really exists.

If the question is as to whether good music has been written by native Americans, I am ready to defend our position. It is in the smaller forms that the American composer is asserting the American individuality most decidedly.

The "Witches' Dance," by MacDowell, is one of the best-known and most genial piano pieces of modern times. The author is alike celebrated in Europe and his own country as one of our leading composers. He is not fully appreciated, and a few years ago he resigned from his position at Columbia University, owing to the unreasonable attitude of the officials.

When we look back and see what has already been accomplished, we surely have every reason to feel hopeful for the high place the American composers should ultimately take. Let us at least recognize their present worth, and do all we can to help them achieve their rightful position in the front ranks of creative workers.

WITCHES' DANCE [Hexentanz]

E. A. MAC DOWELL, Op. 17 [No. 2]

A Lesson on Mendelssohn's Boat Song in A Minor

by Victor Biart
[March 1926]

A gondola gliding indolently over the placid waters of Venice—the City of Canals—bearing, perhaps, a daughter of sunny Italy, basking in the dreamy atmosphere of a summer evening; at the helm a brawny oarsman singing his song to the rhythmical cadence of the stroke of his oars: this picture which, painted in tones, constitutes the barcarolle or Venetian gondolier song. Its basic element is rhythm, the illustrative agency in the musical portrayal of motion. The regular cadence of the movement of the oars corresponds to the recurrent accents on the beginnings of groups of beats. The barcarolle (Ital. *barca*, rowboat) is usually in 6/8 measure, a primary accent falling on the first beat, a secondary or lighter one on the fourth beat. The rhythmic charm of the barcarolle is scarcely less than the tunefulness inevitable in music originating in Italy, that land of eternal melody. This type of composition is admirably adapted to moods that require a short piece for their expression, such as the dreamy, the contemplative, and their kindred. Furthermore the descriptive charm of the illustration of motion and the portrayal of water plays on the imagination of the hearer and stirs the fancy of the romantic composer.

After Mendelssohn's triumphant visit to England in 1829, followed by a pleasure trip to Scotland, the fruits of which later were his sparkling concert overture "Fingal's Cave" and his "Scotch Symphony," he undertook a journey to Italy, in 1830, under the spell of which land more than one composer has come, before and after him. The greatest inspiration of this visit was his "Italian Symphony." But by no means of minor significance are the Venetian gondola songs—those exquisite little compositions that can never age, because they spring from that source of immortality in music, spontaneity. For this reason they have endured after many works more pretentious—including operas and symphonies—have gathered the dust of oblivion. These gondola songs are among the gems contained in that collection of piano classics—classics of romanticism—the *Songs without Words*.

The third gondola song does not date from the composer's first visit to Italy, it is true; the time of its composition is not known, but is believed by some authorities to have been 1842-3. The minor mode, chosen for the first three gondola songs, gives them a certain somberness that adds to the charm of the Venetian coloring. This imparts a somewhat wistful touch to these charming lyrics—for lyrics they are, because of their contemplative character. At the same time they are descriptive miniatures, for they illustrate placid waters and the rhythmical motion of the boat. In form they are the essence of that clarity that points to the classical education of their highly cultured author.

Analysis

An analysis of the third gondola song will reveal at once its structure, namely that of three part song form, the third part being an abridged return of Part I—in this piece, as not infrequently, reduced to a single phrase. The customary repeats are also made. The piece will also be readily seen to be laid out in regular four-measure phrases, with an interludial measure inserted between the end of Part I and its repetition, and between Parts II and III, the latter two being repeated as a unit. Their repetition shows a slightly altered accompaniment in the alto part, in form of syncopation, which heightens the activity and may correspond to increased motion of the water.

Each of the three fundamental elements of music plays its part in the composition of this piece: harmony, maintained by means of the damper pedal, represents the mass of water; rhythm, with its recurrent accents on the first and fourth beats in the accompaniment, describes the gently renewed impulses of the oars and consequent movement of the boat; the song and expressional element, finally, are vested in melody.

An introductory phrase reveals the functions of harmony and rhythm, producing the body of sound or tonal substance in the regular rhythmic cadence of the 6/8 measure. This accompanimental figure underlies the entire piece. A vocative motive in the treble of the second measure, repeated an octave lower in mm. 3 and 4 in reverse metre, calls forth the melody, which begins with the Antecedent of Part I. The soft melody, subdued in its crepuscular *pianissimo*, moving in double-notes, mostly thirds, like two strands, is exquisitely tender. Like a little wash of the water against the boat is the group of graces interjected into m. 7. The semi-cadence reached on the first beat of m. 8 brings the phrase to its inconclusive end and calls forth the consequent phrase, which gives its answer. A new light is revealed as the melody rises to G in m. 10—the climax of the phrase and of the period—illuminated by the dominant and tonic harmonies of the bright relative major key. Quite contrasting with this is the gentle poignancy produced by the suspensions C and E against the D and F of the accompaniment on the first beat of m. 11 and the touch of sadness of the fourth beat. The ending of the period is tastefully rounded off by the vocative motive from the introduction. What a charm the bright coloring produces through the treatment of the melody in combined octaves and thirds in the repetition of this part!

A bond of unity between this and the second part is the series of ascending thirds with which the latter begins in the second half of m. 21. Its similarity to the corresponding portion of m. 5 may suggest community of origin. Like a new stanza is Part II, which plainly represents a new phase of the subject. No feature occasions this more than the dominant harmony to which the graceful and happy melody swings on the accented portion of each measure of the antecedent phrase. The harmonic cadence, joining that of the rhythm, emphasizes the element of motion underlying the piece.

The Climax

The consequent phrase contains the climax of the piece, reached in m. 29. The impulsive ascent of melody and accompaniment through this phrase affords an outlet to the emotional stress and expansion which are the natural culmination of the expressional element. Hence the accents and crescendo which lead to the climax. The chord of the diminished-seventh which is the harmonic basis of this climax, produces what may be termed an open ending; that is, instead of concluding the piece with Part II, it calls forth the tonic harmony, into which it resolves and which, by functioning as a basis of recommencement, introduces Part III. The introductory purpose of this harmony (tonic), ushering in a part instead of concluding one, is particularly indicated by the retention of the fifth (E) in the bass and the holding of its root (A) in abeyance until the fourth measure of this phrase (m. 35).

Attention is invited to the admirable manner in which the connection of Part II to Part III is effected. The climactic effect of m. 29 is preserved by extending the duration of the harmony—the chord of the diminished seventh—two measures further, so as to avoid too abrupt an ending of Part II. Even melodic activity is maintained during this brief interlude by the appearance beneath the accompaniment of the little vocative motive from the introduction, though now so modified as to fit the harmony. The flowing continuity of these two measures produces an aquatic effect of delightful descriptive character.

Of great charm is the unexpected close of the repetition of Parts II and III (as a whole) in the tonic major key in m. 49, producing an effect of pleasant surprise. In this agreeable manner Part III is linked with the coda, the first phrase of which employs for its subject matter the antecedent phrasè of Part II. In the radiant brightness of the key of A major the next phrase runs in flowing 16th-notes up in treble, to meander downwards to the end of the piece, during which latter process the little vocative motive appears in the left hand part in happy retrospect.

How to Render the Piece

The fundamental requisites of the artistic rendering of this piece are the maintenance of rather strict time and a flowing tone. In but few instances are fluctuations of tempo permissible. The introductory phrase should be in strict time, for it indicates the illustrative character and purpose of the piece. There is here no emotional stress to prompt any departure from the tempo, regularity of which is, moreover, essential to the cadence of rowing. Without a tone as above described, every note will sound hard and percussive. This piece can, therefore, serve as a most opportune study for a liquid, fluent tone. To this end the fingers should be held so loose and relaxed as to depress the keys gently. This will allow the tone to flow out of the instrument, so to speak. The beginning should, of course, be the softest possible, yet the first and fourth beats in the accompaniment, which mark the stroke of the oars and stand out as rhythmical salients, should be given a somewhat brighter shade of tone color. The little vocative motive in m. 2 will be loud enough at *forte*. If it be appreciated how soft, yet resplendent, the melody must be then only will the difficulty of the place in the matter of touch and tone production be realized. Moreover, the lower strand of the melody (corresponding to an alto) should be subordinated to the upper line (soprano). By applying to every rise of the melody a gentle crescendo and to each fall a diminuendo, justice will be done to the tone coloring so necessary in this piece. The poise that resides in the longer notes requires that they be well held out— that the accompaniment be not allowed to hurry them. Particular attention is called to the necessity of carrying the crescendo at the end of m. 5 to a bright culmination on the peak of the melody, which, in this phrase, is reached on the first beat of the following measure. Measure 7 is rather difficult of proper treatment, on account of the series of grace-notes. The first of these should begin on the fourth beat. They must then be executed rapidly enough to bring the A of this beat in due time. Yet each note should be clearly audible. In order to avoid interruption of the flow of the melody, hold the A and C of the third beat as long as possible. An entirely different tone quality, again, is required for the series of grace-notes, namely, one of translucent clarity and softness, so that they merely ripple against the melody notes F♯ and A of the fourth beat. The phrase will be well rounded off by a slight broadening of the end of m. 7 and the first half of m. 8, which will bring the semi-cadence, in which some may read an interrogation, into due evidence as the end of the phrase.

An incisive touch on the fourth beat E of m. 8 will, likewise, make it felt that the new phrase begins with this note. The climax of the period, reached on the G of m. 10, can be fully brought out only by means of a crescendo of greater proportions than hitherto attained. Let this note, therefore, ring out clearly and strong, and the eighth-notes rising towards it in the alto not be allowed to overshadow it— nor to be hurried. This dominating point is followed by an abatement as the melody descends to the close of Part I. Within the course of the

diminuendo a slight but effusive accent on the emotionally active first and fourth beats of m. 11—and a gentle lingering on them—will bring out their full expressiveness. To this, as well as to the illumination of the rich harmony of the first beat of this measure, due dynamic fullness of the accompaniment in the left hand on the D and F will contribute materially. A little broadening at the perfect cadence and, particularly, the careful holding out of the A in the melody of m. 12, will, as at the end of the antecedent, enable the hearer to recognize and feel that the sentence here ends. This way the phrase will have been perfectly molded. In order not to dispel the repose of this ending, an infinitesimal delay of the vocative motive which follows is permissible. Admirable playing, indeed, is that which brings out in full the beauty of the silvery coloring of the three strands in which the melody is woven in the repetition of Part I.

About Part II

The fresh impulse with which Part II begins is best reflected in a prompt resumption of the tempo. Even a slight animation will fit the character of this part. A brightening crescendo in the rise of the melody to E in mm. 22 and 24, supported by slightly emphasizing the thirds A and C, and G♯ and B, on the accented beats of the accompaniment, which we have indicated in the music with upturned stems, giving to these notes a certain melodic prominence that emphasizes their rhythmical swing, will add to the vitality of the rendering. The grace-notes in mm. 22 and 24 will be more expressive and tender if not snapped off too short. A little breadth will identify them more with the melody.

The climatic consequent phrase irresistibly actuates an acceleration of tempo conjunctly with as voluminous a crescendo as can well be brought out. The seething of the accompaniment and the all-dominating chord in m. 29 will be more effective if the acceleration is checked in m. 28. More power can be given to the climatic chord in m. 29 by assigning the lowest note (A) of the treble to the left hand. Subsidence of tempo following the vocative motive in m. 30 is the means of mediating from the preceding torrential passage to the soft, peaceful quiet of Part III.

The great dynamic contrast referred to in the analysis requires due attention to the *pianissimo*—not merely *piano*—which must color Part III. The poignancy of the F in the accompaniment of m. 34, falling into the C and E of the treble, offers just the opportunity for the expression of a painful cry. The variety and command of tone color required by this piece are evident in the *pianissimo* demanded for the repetition of Part II, which in its first appearance began merely *piano*. The syncopated Es in the alto add greatly to the flowing character of the music. To produce the liquid quality of tone essential to this, the thumb should be dropped lightly and gently to the key, rather than made to strike it actively. Here, again, the slight prominence to be given to the first and fourth beats of the accompaniment is recommended.

The softer shade of dynamics here necessary to correspond to that of the treble will reveal anew this popular composer in his capacity as a delightful colorist, and will bring to the realization of many the fact that these pieces are not so easy to render with true artistry.

The return of Part III will be observed to be indicated *p—pp*. This latter shade is reserved for the coda and is offset by the brightness of the major mode in which the piece ends with typical Romantic cheerfulness.

With aquatic fluency, soft and with flowing legato, the 16th-note passage of the closing phrase should ripple along to the end. A slight lingering on the first note of the vocative motive, which twice calls back pleasantly in the left hand, involving an infinitesimal broadening of the arpeggio undulating above it, will impart a touch of affectionate and fitting gentleness to this simple but lovely melodic bit.

VENETIAN BOAT-SONG

F. MENDELSSOHN, Op. 62, No. 5

Repetition of Part III

Coda

A Master Lesson for Earnest Students

Mendelssohn's Charming "Spinning Song"

Analyzed and Interpreted by the Distinguished Polish Virtuoso and Composer

SIGISMUND STOJOWSKI

[November 1916]

The great Belgian poet [Emile] Verhaeren [1855-1916] says that to classify art and artists is like trying "to fix the shape of a passing cloud." Classification has, indeed, too often miscarried as science, and art-criticism has, occasionally, shown overambitious "scientific" pretenses. It remains true, nevertheless, that the human mind, in its pursuit of knowledge, needs help itself, in presence of the overwhelming task that confronts it, by grouping facts and things in a spirit of orderliness, according to resemblances perceived and set definitions. These well may be, in matters as subtle as art, either too simple or too vague. Even so, we pack our stock of information into the "innovation-trunks" of our brains—where the complexity of things is perhaps ill at ease, but where the various compartments help the carrying-power of our memory and understanding.

The so-called "romantic" spirit pervades a whole group of composers, to which Mendelssohn emphatically belongs and who, because of an unmistakable classical learning, seem to stand on the borderland and may perhaps be fittingly described as "romantic-classics" or "classical-romanticists." To forms brought to perfection by their classical ancestors they cling with a faithfulness that implies imitation, or they stumble in helplessness. Of the later, Mendelssohn is never guilty. No innovator and breaker of barriers, he is a great master in actual achievement.

Felix Mendelssohn loved flowers and fairies. Reciprocally, flowers seemed to gather in a soft carpet for his walk of life and the good fairies evidently assembled at his cradle to bestow rare gifts upon that elect of their heart. To his muse they imparted something of their own grace, lightness and fluidity and his art was to have the fragrant naturalness of flowers blooming in the sun. A quality of perennial youth, with all of its happy vivacity, seems inherent to Mendelssohn. For that very reason his art never fails to beguile the sympathy of the young ones—although it many a time is irresistible to any age—while its flawless craftsmanship commands unreserved admiration. Not only generous and discriminating Schumann, but all contemporaries worshipped the skill and knowledge of this master, and lovingly responded to his nature's charm and serenity, beneath which they felt deep-seated goodness, spiritual harmony and lofty idealism. Posterity, whose verdicts are not necessarily as just and true as we are prone to believe, has gone too far in the opposite direction, in minimizing Mendelssohn's merits and, which is worse, in neglecting his works. To one critic "his elfs look like flies"—another thinks the Spinning Song "tied on wire." We hardly ever hear his oratorios, symphonies and overtures any more. Yet Wagner himself held *The Hebrides* the most perfect orchestral piece in existence.

The "Songs Without Words"

Pierre Loti [1850-1925], the writer, another gentle and masterly poet, asserts that any sincere artist is born with one or two songs on his lips, which he goes on repeating. This should suffice if the song only be truly one's own. In Mendelssohn's case it was mostly a "Song Without Words"—whether called so or not. But then the name and the thing wholly belong to him. Models of that form can, of course, he found. Yet the Beethovenian Andante from which some critics make it derive, has an altogether different character, a greater breadth in both conception and treatment. But Mendelssohn's *Andante* from the Violin-Concerto is, in its very inception, a "Song Without Words."

And a certain condensation of form—for all of its variety and perfect logic—distinguishes that Mendelssohnian creation from all "the chips of the great workshops" of others [reference to William H. Hadow 1859-1937. See also p. 105]. There are eight books of these "songs" for the piano, written at different periods and obviously serving the same purpose for which, once upon a time, old John Sebastian contributed to art his so-called *Galanterien:* to provide some wholesome food and entertainment to the student and lover of music.

Rubinstein justly remarks that these songs were meant to supplant in the homes the nauseating literature of operatic transcriptions and tasteless variations which at the time encumbered the concert-halls. The standard, accordingly, to judge of their value and service to art, should be the historical one. They both lose and gain by it, however. They lose when compared with the passionate outbursts of greater and bolder contemporaries, the "Preludes" of a Chopin, the *Fantasiestücke* of a Schumann. But they immeasurably gain if we consider the average literature of the period! Quantity however, is the sworn enemy of quality, alas!—and in art, as the cruelly witty French writer [Nicholas de] Chamfort [1741-1791] has it: "facility is a wonderful gift, provided it be not used." Perfection of form too, occasionally spells some coolness—and on the whole, one may subscribe to Mr. [Edward] Dannreuther's [1844-1905] judgment that most of those little pieces, intended to be simple and straightforward and almost Mozartian in the expression of emotion, so full of pleasing grace, so refined and well-balanced in workmanship, are "not music in the warmest sense of the word." Yet they contain some gems like the tenderly serene one in G (No. 25), the nobly beautiful in F (No. 22), the joyously exuberant "Hunting Song", the daintily vivacious "Spinning Song." These can indeed be loved as much as they should be admired and studied.

Harmony and Euphony; Color and Form

The piano-technique of Mendelssohn who was a wonderful pianist himself, is voluntarily sober, reflects the musician rather than the virtuoso. It only utilizes the previously existing resources, the material accumulated in the works of other masters, without reaching out into the realm of new and richer complexities. Of empty virtuosity it is void—but those strokes of genius in pianistic invention which have so characteristically marked the style of a Chopin or Liszt, are absent too. The master of the instrument is mostly felt in a certain euphony, which, however, in all of Mendelssohn's art has been a matter of principle. His harmony could be defined along the same lines: there are none of these novel and rich "finds" that abound in Chopin—only naturalness and discrimination, bordering on conventionality, marred by occasional weakness due mostly to the ample use of diminished sevenths. The instrumental setting and harmonic scheme are the two factors which form, combined, what we are used to calling, and perceiving as, color in music. While distinctly conservative, Mendelssohn was a great master in color. A comparison between old and new ideals in this order of things is indeed profitable.

Modern art more and more disregards euphony and even harmony, in its irrepressible search after rich or merely peculiar color. A master-colorist of the romantic period, which Mendelssohn assuredly was, rigorously subjected the color-scheme to the musical law of euphony, the former being really made dependent on the latter. Nor was the line and design, which we in the narrower sense call form in music, ever sacrificed by him. It was in this that he well-nigh reached the absolute. Biographers tell us that Mendelssohn—a man of versatile gifts and broad culture—was sensitive to nature and highly proficient in drawing. Translate this into musical terms and you perhaps find the secret of that exquisite balance, which even now, in these times of deliberate formlessness, compels the admiration of the art-student and, perhaps, his jealousy. For what is art if not order put into the chaos of matter and thought?

The Spinning-Song

Just glance at the perfect linear proportion of this little "Spinning-Song"—and then realize how richly colored it is in its hustling and rushing euphony. Although wonderfully pianistic, the various tints of a many-hued orchestral palette are felt throughout by an imaginative ear. Two measures of introduction in which the united violins—or violas—mutter a swiftly moving design suggestive of the spinning wheel—then, while this motion is persistently going on, a melody sets in, gently hummed, in short notes, underlined by violins "pizzicato," reflecting, as it were, the happy mood of the spinning girls, so characteristically the composer's own. It is easy also to imagine how Mendelssohn would have played this dainty little piece himself, if we look up testimonials of contemporaries who heard him play. Listen to Bishop Grower: "His hands on the keys behaved like living and intelligent creatures full of life and sympathy." And Joachim testifies that "his staccato was the most extraordinary thing possible for life and crispness."

Now this little piece is all grace, lightness and vivacity. Naturally limber wrists and agile fingers are a primary condition needed for an adequate performance. Much of the effect, however, is dependent upon fingering. While fingering, of course, is not an absolute matter and allowances have to be constantly made for individual possibilities and conveniences, yet the editor believes in the virtue of some rational system—in this as, in fact, in every human attainment. One cue is, for instance, the avoidance of the repetition of the same finger on frequently recurring notes in quick movement. (See the application at (**1**)) It secures ease and brilliancy, while the reverse engenders heaviness and lameness. Nor should the performer shun a fingering which, at first sight, seems uncomfortable, if it be conducive to greater security, as, for instance, the passing under of the thumb onto the G at (**3**). Tailors and boot-makers tell us, that the test of a good fit is its ease, but this, really, only shows in the wearing! To secure that passage, some exercises of the following kind are recommended:

In the following repeat exercise (A) several times and then add notes as in (B) and (C). Practice slowly and mind the accents.

This means reverting to the basic principles of arpeggio-technique. But it is serviceable and manly—in art as well as in life—to "take the bull by the horns" as the familiar saying and rare deed are!

The key of the dominant reached in this very passage indicates the end of the first member of the musical phrase. Its second member starts in—at **B**—on the dominant seventh which firmly reestablishes the initial key. We notice that this section is conceived and constructed differently from the first one. The melodic notes succeed one another

in even rhythm, and repetition of the new motive of two bars—then of one bar derived from it—becomes a factor of development which leads to another, partly novel bit of melody in G major (**C**). To have that melody clearly outlined one has to accent the melodic notes liable to be covered up by the accompaniment—at (**5**), (**6**), and (**7**).

To this section which plays—because of the key relationship and place it occupies—the part of a miniature "second theme"—the initial design of the introduction is affixed. It is harmonized this time and extended—through a charming echo-like effect—to lead back to the main theme (**D**). The editor suggests refraining from the use of the damper-pedal and using, on the contrary, the soft pedal on that echo (**8**). For the sake of contrast he has marked one pedal for the two previous bars—which is perhaps not rigorously catholic, but coloristically effective.

The initial phrase is now repeated (**D**), but not in its entirety. It breaks off into a new—but derived—sequential development (**E**). Two bars in the key of the subdominant, followed by two bars in the key of the tonic lead to a short, joyously bubbling climax (**9**), which by a gracefully witty turn—a clarinet-solo—falls back again, down to a whisper and concludes on the tonic (**11**). Let us again remove the pedal, for the sake of character, at (**10**)—and leave that dainty clarinet solo only supported by short chords—strings "pizzicato," as it were.

Up to this point the musical contents of the piece have been completed. What follows only repeats, develops and rounds out—in a way that plainly shows the composer's ingeniousness. Section **F** introduces for the first time, the minor mode, which carries a new flavor into this already known fragment, absolutely parallel to **B**. Section **C** is reproduced in turn by **G**—this time in the more distant key of E major. What has been said before of this little melody, applies to the corresponding places here ((**12**), (**13**), and (**14**) as compared with (**5**), (**6**), and (**7**)). The introduction now starts in on new intervals (**14**) and leads, through chromatic sequences, back to the original key. Again, the previously made remarks about pedaling with regard to well-contrasted shadings, are valid here. It should be noticed how—through a happy condensation—the last echo-like passage (**17**) appears one step higher, which imparts a fresh impression while it shortens the road home. The composer's notation at (**15**) and (**16**) need not be taken too rigorously, the additional notes merely squeezed in so that the duration of each group remains identical, each bar being divided into two groups consistently.

Section **H** brings back **D** and **E** up to the close, that close being this time emphasized by repetition, with heightened dynamic effect (**18**), thus preparing the coda of the whole piece. This coda really consists of two segments: **I** and **J**. The first is closely—and very logically—related to the beginning of the song and might be described as the coda of the song itself. The second prolongs the piece through the accompanying design, carries a reminder of the echo-like effect (**19**), this time the fundamental of the tonic underlying it—and finally merges into a brisk little ascending run (**20**); a pianistically effective close. The shading crescendo marked on that run apparently belongs to the composer, since it is reproduced in all editions. This writer, however, prefers to have the crescendo in the middle of the run and to let it then expire in a dainty *pp* at the top. There are in music expression-marks that are binding, so to speak intrinsic; others, on the contrary, may be subject to change in accordance with the taste of the performer, whose highest duty is to "recreate" the music. For this a certain measure of liberty must be allowed him up to a point; his insight must be trusted as complementary to the composer's more or less accurate directions—if only he keeps in mind the warning: "traduttore-tradstore" [see also p. 101].

SPINNING SONG

Edited and fingered by S. Stojowski

F. MENDELSSOHN, Op. 67, No. 4

AN INTERPRETATION LESSON ON
Mozart's "Fantasia in D-Minor"
Prepared by
J O H N   O R T H

[May 1914]

Every piece of music is what you make of it. In this lesson I want to help you to make all you can of this beautiful work. Let me quote here my favorite thought from Wagner [from H. T. Finck [1854-1926], *Success in Music and How it is Won;* 1909, p. 428]:

> "Wagner, as just stated, counseled his artists to ignore the division of music into regular bars. 'After the singer has completely absorbed my intentions,' he added, 'let him freely follow his own feelings, even to the physical demands of breathing in agitated passages; and the more *independent and creative* his *emotional abandon* makes him, the more he will excite my admiration and wonder.' How far all this takes us away, not from expression itself— for the improvisational style of singing and playing is that very inner secret and perfection of expression we have been seeking for—but, from mere printed expression *marks*, which are only a crude approximation to what a great artist makes of a piece! As a rule, even these are not attended to, and then performers wonder why high-class concerts do not pay as well as vaudeville and musical comedy! They would pay equally well if the high-class music were as adequately interpreted as the low-class usually is. There's the truth in a nutshell."

Now, this is the spirit in which I wish you to approach this piece. In order to do so, you must be thoroughly relaxed in mind and body.

Special Pedal Study
Place your hands on the keys and play the first measure with a heavy devitalized hand and finger. Hold the pedal during the first two measures; retard at the end of the first measure. Think of the second measure as an echo. If you have imagination, give it full play. Fill your mind with thoughts of sounds reverberating over the hills and mountains. Listen, and delay an instant after the first measure. Then play the next measure in a dreamy *pianissimo* manner. Listen again! Keep your foot on the pedal during these two measures and hear the wonderful pedal effect! Anton Rubinstein said: "The more I play, the more thoroughly I am convinced that the pedal is the soul of the piano; there are cases where the pedal is everything." Do not think yet of m. 3. Let your hand lie upon the keys until the reverberation grows dim. Let the left hand lie upon the octave D, while the right hand clings to the last four notes of the measure.

In every measure there are, what I call *expression notes,* which, as a rule, should be delayed and lingered upon a little. This is the way that the first six measures should be treated: m. 3, loud and relaxed; m. 4 echo, *pianissimo*; again, wait, listen and imagine. Measure 5, loud and relaxed. Measure 6, after a little pause, echo, *pianissimo*. Linger upon the octave in the left hand and the last three or four notes in the right hand. In these six measures do not leave the keys with either hand. Play as if your hands sank into the

keys and as if they had no more spring to them than a jellyfish. Play mm. 1, 3, and 5 at about 60 quarter notes. Measures 2, 4 and 6 a little slower with a retard at the end of the measures.

The significant notes in the next two measures are the half notes in the left hand. Keep your hands limp. Play these half notes with a full, firm touch. Raise the fingers from the eighth and quarter notes so that the only sounds that are heard are the half notes in the left hand. Listen! See how full and rich the tone is in this register of the piano. Don't think anything about *time*. Just listen and imagine that you are producing a fine tone on a cello. Treat the four half notes in these two measures, 7 and 8, in the same manner. Use no pedal. Pay no attention to the ties in the right hand.

In m. 9 play the first note lightly and solidly; then with a heavy tread climb up the hill. In turning around at the top "slow up" slightly; linger a bit on the D♯; then meander on to the end of m. 10 with a little lighter step. Retard a little at the end of the measure. Hold the pedal through these two measures, 9 and 10.

Take the A in m. 11 *forte*, with a firm touch, without the pedal. Hold it. At the end of two beats put on the pedal. Release the hand and listen. This is one of the richest notes on the keyboard. Give it plenty of time—at least four beats after putting on the pedal. Hold the pedal until the first note of m. 12, so that there is no break in the sound.

Expression Notes
Notice that from here on it is marked *Adagio*. This is one of the most plaintive of melodies, full of feeling and expression. In cantabile passages of this kind there are always *expression notes*. The important note, or expression note in this measure is G in the right hand. Give this note a little extra attention. Linger on it a bit as if loath to leave it. Don't overdo it. Make it about half as long again as written. An eighth note can be stretched, so to speak, to three-sixteenths, but never to four-sixteenths, because then it is a quarter note, and that won't do.

In m. 13 the expression note is D♯. Linger on that. Make it about three-sixteenths in value. Give it a little more poignancy than any other note in the measure, by making all the other notes *pianissimo*, accenting and lingering upon the D♯. Half steps are amongst the most expressive intervals in music. That is why the D♯–E in m. 13 is much more expressive than the interval G–F in m. 12, or the same interval in m. 14. In m. 14 delay on A in the right hand.

In m. 15 delay on G. In m. 16 we have a half step in the right hand and two half steps in the left hand, from D to C♯ and F to E. Be very firm on the A in the right hand and on the D in the left hand. Let these two voices oppose each other with a touch of anguish. When a wail is suggested in music it is most always done by means of chromatic passages.

Measure 17 has a touch of wail in it. Don't think of tempo when you play this measure. Think of wail and make it sound like one. You will play it approximately in time, of course. But don't think of time, think wail. Measures 17 and 18 go wailing and sobbing on, as you see. It is all half steps, chromatic. Play with a heavy hand, a heavy heart and a heavy tread.

In m. 19 die into a whisper. Again, don't think of time. Let this measure pass off into the clouds, noiselessly. Put on the pedal, of course, with the first note. Hold it two measures until the sound has nearly disappeared.

The hero of the play now appears. In the next two measures 20 and 21 he makes himself felt and heard with abundant vitality and a stentorian voice. The first note in m. 22 is very firm. Then all melts away into a whisper.

The next three measures suggest palpitation, agitation. We will imagine it is the heroine speaking. Does she say "To-morrow, To-morrow, To-morrow" and so on?

Measure 26 is still more agitated. Ritard much at the end of this measure and two notes on m. 27. After these first two notes the agitation and tempo increase and come to an abrupt conclusion at the end of the measure.

At m. 29 our plaintive yearning theme enters again, as in m. 12, only in another key. The expression note in this measure is D. In m. 30 it is A♯ against B in the left hand (very poignant). In m. 31 it is G against G♯ in the left hand (also very poignant). In m. 32 D♯, and in m. 33 F♯ against E, and C against C♯, are the notes of expression. Ritard on the last two notes of m. 33 and wait.

We come now to a real musical flourish. Even this must not be done superficially. There are expression notes. Linger an instant on each of the four Cs going down. Stop an instant on the lowest C. Put on the pedal. Take as grand a sweep as you can to the top note E♭. Keep the pedal down until these eighteen notes die away. This is a beautiful pedal effect. Make the most of it.

Read again what Rubinstein says about the Pedal. Do this flourish as fast as you can. Don't scramble.

Hero and Heroine
In m. 35 our hero enters again, strong and virile as before in m. 20, remaining with us during the next two measures, 36 and 37. Our heroine is with us during the next six measures 38–43 inclusive. Her palpitation and agitation rise to a higher pitch than before in mm. 23–27 inclusive. Ritard at the end of m. 43 and wait.

In the next flourish, m. 44, delay a little on the first note. Ritard a

little at the beginning of the three succeeding groups, on B♭, A, C. Be very firm on the low A and the following A. Go slowly on the next three sixteenths. Put on the pedal on the next eighth note A. Hold the pedal until you get to the last four notes of this chromatic scale. Ritard a little on these last four notes. Be sure to keep your finger on the half note A until you reach Tempo I.

From here on to m. 51 inclusive, is the same as mm. 12–17 inclusive.

In m. 52 there are two expression notes—A and E.

In m. 53 the first note—E.

In m. 54 we have another splendid pedal effect in thirty-second notes. There are sixteen of them. Hold the pedal until they die away.

Play the two chords in m. 55 light and dry. No pedal.

A Delightful Finale
The Allegretto is peaceful. No more stress or agitation. The first expression note is the first note in m. 57. These first eight measures are lighthearted, almost gay in spirit. Let your touch be of the same nature.

The next eight measures are a little more serious and legato. Bring out the Tenor part in m. 65. Pause a little before m. 70, as if there were a comma. Ritard a little in mm. 70 and 71.

From here on to m. 88 play in the most lighthearted manner, almost as frolicsome as a little child. Ritard a little on m. 79. In m. 88 hold the pedal from the first note until you get to the top of the hill D. Make a long trill on E with a diminuendo at the end.

From here on to m. 100 inclusive, sweet and light as in the first eight measures. Whisper mm. 101–104. Play them a little slower. Play the last six measures briskly and peppery. No pedal.

Harold Bauer [1873-1951] says: "I am strongly convinced that too much time is spent on the externals of piano playing and not enough in reaching the heart of the matter. It is the end that counts, not the means, especially if the means are of such a character as will never take one to the end."

I want you to look upon this as a lesson in expression; in the technic of expression. Catch the spirit back of it all and all will be well with you and your interpretation.

How I Gave My First Lesson
A Symposium of Particular Interest to Your Teachers and Students Who Aspire to be Teachers.
John Orth
[July 1912]

The thought of writing to THE ETUDE always gives me a thrill of pleasure, because I know its readers are many and brainy.

The first lesson I gave on the piano could not have been of much value. In fact the first lessons I gave were on the flute, when I was ten years old, to a young fellow who thought I knew it all and proposed that I play the tunes on the piano, while he tried to follow on the flute. I agreed; he was satisfied, and I was glad to get my "fifty cents a lesson" to save up to go to Liszt, which I began to do about that time.

My father, a German, placed me on a piano stool when I was eight. The first year I practiced an hour a day on the first page of Schmidt's five-finger exercises, the next year two hours a day on the same page and the scale of C. The third year my practice time was three hours a day, and I was allowed a bit more liberty, but only in the direction of music in its strictest form. I was caught one day playing the "Soldier's Joy", a capital offence for which I was disgraced and duly punished. In my twelfth year I began to teach,

I was glad to receive fifty cents a lesson at this time, but what did I know about teaching? I had been kept down to an eternal, infernal grind and that's all I knew about it. I was asked to teach and was ready. I believe one should never refuse a request of that sort. Better to try and fail than not to dare. Do what you are afraid to do. Fear is the great enemy; conquer it at all cost.

My first piano pupil was about thirty years old. She brought me a stack of music about a foot high. I was nearly scared to death, and I think she felt pretty uncomfortable too. See Shakespeare's *As You Like It,* Act I, Scene 2. I finally selected Richardson's *New Method* and we started in. Had she been a child, it would have been different. You see I was in doubt as to what to do, because of my responsibility as a teacher of one so much older.

I think no teacher is ever quite free from a certain amount of trepidation with every new pupil, for there are no two alike. He must adapt his knowledge to their needs and natures, and therein lies the art of teaching.

FANTASIA
IN D-MINOR

W. A. MOZART
Revised by S. Lebert

+) *mp mezzo piano*, somewhat soft signifies
a degree of shading which stands between *p* and *mf*.

✢) These four measures *pp* may be played somewhat more quietly than the previous Allegretto Tempo requires, but with
the following *f* the regular Tempo will take its place again. Still, care must be taken that this slight deviation from strict
time is not carried to excess, for under no circumstances should it form a contrast between dragging and hurrying.

Paderewski's Minuet in G

How the Composer and His Famous Colleagues Interpret It

By JOHN ROSS FRAMPTON
Professor of Piano Playing at Oberlin Conservatory

[December 1923]

The printed notation is at best a very inadequate and rather cumbersome means of depicting a composer's intentions. Moreover there are little things which add to the interest of a composition, but which the composer has never incorporated in the printed version. It is therefore especially fortunate when we have his own interpretation recorded; and doubly so when the composer is at the same time the world's greatest master of his instrument.

This article is based on a study of two different performances of the Minuet made by Mr. Paderewski about 1911 (Victor, No. 88321) and 1917 (Victor, No. 74533), the earlier of which is no longer in the catalogue. Reference will also be made to the only other records of this piece as piano solo, one by Mr. Josef Hofmann (Columbia A No. 5915) and one by Mr. Rudolf Ganz (Pathe, No. 59055), the present conductor of the St. Louis Orchestra.

General Tempo

Even the most superficial listener to these records will notice the difference in general tempo. Mr. Hofmann [1876-1957], whose art inclines to the brilliant, played at 160, taking three and one-half minutes for the entire piece. Mr. Ganz [1877-1972] played at the tempo indicated, ♩=144. The earlier Paderewski record is at ♩=138 and requires four minutes; while the latest Paderewski is at ♩= 126 and takes four and a half minutes, and is thus almost a third longer than the Hofmann performance. Mr. Ganz omitted the repeats, so his entire time is short. Mr. Paderewski, as always, varies much in tempo, from measure to measure, dropping below 126 and even reaching 200, but always returning to 126 as his normal. (These tempi were determined by the metronome, after tuning the records to the pitch of the piano. Mr. [Henry T.] Finck writes that the thing in which Paderewski surpasses every other pianist is in that he never fails to make the entire audience enjoy any beauty spot, but lingers lovingly on all such. [*Success in Music and How it is Won*, 1909, p. 316.])

Motifs

Composers often add to the coherence, unity and interest of a composition by the employment of some *motif*; that is, by some very short melodic phrase, in either the melody or the accompaniment, or by some striking turn of the harmony, which recurs repeatedly through the work. It is probable that in many cases the composer did not analyze his own work enough to realize that his mind had subconsciously incorporated such a motif. There is generally no attempt to indicate such motifs in the printed notation, and the performer endeavors to find them and emphasize them discreetly. In the Minuet records Mr. Ganz apparently did not attempt any motivation. Both the other pianists did, but they chose different motifs.

Mr. Hofmann used the six notes of the turn (∾) in the main theme (Ex. 1a).

Ex. 1 (a) (b) (c)

He plays them very fast, and with a sharp accent on the first note, reminding one of the buzz with which the airplane motor starts. Incidentally, whenever the turn leads from a higher to a lower note (as in mm. 1 and 3), he merely trills, not playing the undernote in the turn at all (Ex. 1b). He starts the chain trills of the coda with a similar buzz, and ends the long trill in the middle section (the trio), in the same way, using as motif the last three notes of the trill, the grace note C♯ and the first note of the theme (Ex. 1c).

Mr. Hofmann can almost be said to use a second motif, the two grace notes and the G in m. 5 (Ex. 2a).

Ex. 2 (a) (b)

He accents the top note but does not play the grace notes extremely fast; in fact, he caresses them a trifle in m. 6 and other measures. By starting the turn with the buzz and then accenting the last notes and slightly delaying them, he combines both motifs in the fourth measure of the theme whenever it recurs, especially in the loud part between the left hand octaves and the ascending scale in sixteenth notes (Ex. 2b). He does not seem to apply this motif to the grace notes in the trio, even though they catch the eye instantly by their similarity in appearance to the motif as printed in m. 5. Possibly he feels that the motif would call for more brilliancy than would be in keeping with this more melodic portion of the piece; possibly he wished to avoid the jazzy effect which the average student gives to these notes.

Mr. Paderewski used two motifs. His principal motif is the upward skip of an octave as shown in the first two notes of the trio (Ex. 3a).

Ex. 3 (a) (b) (c) (d)

con 8 8 8

He does not make them brilliant, but strong and bold, compelling the hearer's attention. He accents both notes, and makes the lower note long, regardless of the notation. He finds this motif everywhere. In fact he began his earlier record with it, by playing a preliminary thumb D (as a quarter note) before the first printed note. In both records he added a thumb D as grace note (shorter that usual for this motif in the last measure of the first ending (Ex. 3b), playing the (unwritten) right thumb D simultaneously with the low G of the left hand, and the (right) printed D a trifle later. In the measure containing the final D of the left hand octave passage he so motivates the two right hand Ds which enclose the bar-line (Ex. 3c). Here he secures it in part by delaying the second note of the main theme, thus slightly isolating the two notes of the motif. He so motivates the last D of the three times recurring rapidamente cadenza with the D after the bar-line, (the one with the famous fermata). He plays the entire cadenza without ritard and abruptly stops on the last D before the bar-line, holds it as long as he usually holds the first note of the motif, and then plays the upper D (Ex. 3d). He uses the grace notes (G up to G, and F up to F) in the ninth and thirteenth measures of the trio in the same way. In these measures he gives the grace note G as much time as the quarter G at the beginning of the trio: the F he plays a little faster, and he adds a slowly played grace note D (not written) in the seventeenth measure. And finally he so motivates the thumb D, just before the coda, with the first note of the chain trills.

Mr. Paderewski uses as a second motif the three notes G, E, D in the left hand of mm. 7 and 8. This motif will be studied in a later paragraph.

It is interesting that neither artist employs the motifs of the other man. Thus Mr. Paderewski uses the turn (∿) in the theme merely as a melodic bridge between the D and the B, and grades it in power and speed accordingly, decrescendo when descending and vice versa, and always giving it dignity and repose. The other Hofmann *motif* is generally caressed by Mr. Paderewski, and is never made brilliant. On the other hand Mr. Hofmann not only does not use the two-note octave motif of Mr. Paderewski, but he even omits the preliminary G at the trio. He plays the grace notes of this section very fast, (almost like poorly struck octaves) and does not play the unwritten grace note D at the seventeenth measure. His purpose in this section is apparently to strike the grace-notes with sufficient power to make them sing through the tied four measures. Mr. Paderewski depends on the sympathetic vibration from other struck tones to continue the long notes. (Those who are interested in this tonal reinforcement of a held key may find a very remarkable example in the final F in Mr. Paderewski's rendition of his own Nocturne in Bb as recorded in Victor No. 74765, made in 1922.)

Anachronous Interpretation of Ornaments

Mr. Paderewski calls this Minuet "*à l'Antique*," yet he never gives the ornaments the strict interpretation ordained by Emmanuel Bach, the great authority on *agréments* (*Grove's Dictionary*). The strict interpretation of the turn (∿) in the theme would not start on C, but on D, and consist of but four notes (Ex. 4a).

Ex. 4

What every one plays here (Ex. 4c) is the "geschnellte doppelschlag," which would require a grace-note before the C in the notation (Ex. 4b). Probably because it would not sound well otherwise, every one plays the first note of this turn on the count, which is correct.

The two-note graces of m. 5 (Mr. Hofmann's second motif) and of the trio are written as *vorschlaege*. According to Bach the grace-note E should be played simultaneously with the C–E of the left hand, and the F–G of the right hand should come after "three" (Ex. 4d). But every record places the grace notes before "three," and G of the right hand with the left chord on "three" (Ex. 4f), which makes the ornaments become the "*nachschlaege*" of Bach (Ex. 4e). Paderewski uses the usual interpretation of such graces in modern writers.

The grace-note C♯ in m. 9 should sound at the same time as the D, F♯ chord (Ex. 5a) and the C♮ later. This is never done, and Mr. Paderewski

gives a very free interpretation.

Ex. 5

The turns in the left hand (hint at the main theme) at the end of the trio are written in such a way as to demand C♯ as the under note (Ex. 5b). Many editions indicate the rendition of the graces; some print B♮ (Ex. 5b) and some B♯ (Ex. 5c). All four records play B♮. It is noteworthy, in passing, that Mr. Hofmann continues the right-hand trill as in C minor (playing E♭) during these two turns and only changes to E♮ for the last two measures of the trill.

The old-time performance of the grace-note D in m. 13, would place the grace-note simultaneously with the two lower notes of the chord and on the count, the C♮ following later, alone, similar to Ex. 5e, except that he did not play it at all in m. 13 (first time), and possibly not after the first *rapidamente* cadenza.

Cadences

Mr. Paderewski played none of the cadences, except the last, as loud as the other pianists. The first ending, mm. 16 and 17, which occurs but once in the piece, he takes staccato and without ritard. The second ending he plays differently in different places. The first time he spreads the right-hand chord on count "two," doing it fast but not snappily, and also spreads the final chord—in the next measure—slowly and caressingly. At the second appearance of this cadence—after the trio—he spread the last chord fast, also. The varying speeds and powers with which Mr. Paderewski spreads chords, and the way he caresses the melody tones in them, constitute a very special and helpful study, not only in this piece, but also in all his records. In the earlier record he played both the last two chords of the Minuet softly, but in the later record both are loud, and the final low G grace-note receives a full quarter-note time, the chord appearing on count "two."

Mr. Hofmann altered the cadences enough to warrant mention. At the repeat mark before the trio he does not use the cadence written, but plays that of the second ending of the main theme, and accelerates, playing loud to lead into the loud portion which follows. On the repeat—as entrance to the trio—he plays the cadence written, doing it softly, and on count "two" plays only one tone, the soprano note C. In the final cadence he omits the top B of the next to last chord, hardly spreads the chord at all, and replaces the last chord with only G in unison, with the G above middle C as top note.

The Rapidamente Cadenza

This is a very interesting place in the records. Mr. Hofmann kept the first and last appearances of this cadenza without pedal, with a staccato left hand chord to start it, and the cadenza taken very fast, ending softly. The second appearance he ritarded the ascending closing arpeggio and pedaled it somewhat. He evidently tried to render it differently each time.

Mr. Paderewski finds both his motifs in the cadenza! He played it with power throughout, and the last seven notes as loud as possible. Yet he lets the left hand cut through (beginning with the ascending sixteenths two measures before). He, as everywhere, phrases the left hand as shown in Ex. 6, with the first note of each measure serving as last note of the thought, and then picks out the notes of mm. 7 and 8 (his second motif) from among the notes of the cadenza. Both records show this, but the later is a finer conception (Ex. 6 and 7a). It is not easy to bring out the E–D loud, just after the two soft tones, and the piano will not always do it, because of the rebound of the key, so even Mr. Paderewski does not always succeed. He plays the entire cadenza fast, and concludes with the octave motivation, as already explained. He keeps his pedal down throughout the cadenza and lets it up on the half note, after having filled both hands full of keys from the arpeggio somewhat as shown in Ex. 6, which he releases slowly from the bass up. The remarkable singing quality of his tone is again demonstrated by the way the half note D sings after the other keys are released. He plays the grace note C♯ as always. The general effect, after releasing the lower keys and holding the high D alone, is a *largo* tempo to include the first chord of the next measure, and the last two chords played right up to tempo. He waited longer on the C♮ each time the cadenza appeared.

In his earlier record he did not so clearly intend to use the octave motif, but allowed the last note before the bar to be part of the other motif, as shown in Ex. 7b.

Odds and Ends

Mr. Paderewski puts the pedal down on "one" and up on "two," in most of the record, making the chords staccato, and generally accenting count "two" more than "one." The eighths in m. 10 and others, are generally staccato (Ex. 8a). In the loud theme after the left hand octaves his pedal comes up on "three" and down on "one."

The left hand descending passage, after the double bar, starts at about 184 and accelerates in the octaves to 200. The theme which follows drops back to 138 (168 in Hofmann), and he delays on the first note twice its value (end of octave motif), actually placing four ticks of the metronome in this measure once. The trio is back at 126, and with splendidly subdued accompaniment. The earlier record played for several measures almost at ♩=144, but deviated from the intermediate ticks very much a splendid example of rubato.

Some editors indicate the exact number of notes to play in the long trill at the end of the trio, and attempt to show the ritard, even. Mr. Paderewski ritards the left hand very much, but keeps the trill very fast to the end, softening down, and stopping on a soft D, followed by a soft C♯, each held as a slow quarter note. Incidentally we may mention that he plays a D in the left hand under the first group of eighth notes near the beginning of the trill, for five groups.

Mr. Paderewski started the coda in his earlier record at ♩=176, but his later record is only 152 during the trills (thus emphasizing the restraint which has been characteristic of the main theme), increasing to 184 at the triplets. The measure in which the right hand starts down he played without pedal and with a staccato left hand chord in the first record, but in the later record, he kept this chord sustained, both here and four measures later. In the following measure in both places and in both records he played a three-note chord in the left hand, quietly and sustained. (Ex. 8d)

In conclusion may we be permitted to mention one thing which is not supposed to be on the record and which is probable unique in professional recording. All who have attended a Paderewski recital will recall the frequency with which the word "Bravo" is shouted. After the artist finished his performance some man in the recording room was so enthused that he shouted "Bravo" and this word is faintly but distinctly present on the earlier record.

MENUET A L'ANTIQUE

I. J. PADEREWSKI, Op. 14, No. 1

a) **2 3** may be played with the left hand if preferred. This manner of execution facilitates and increases the brilliancy and effect of the passage.

Rubinstein's Barcarolle in F-Minor

Analytical Lesson by the Noted Pianist - Composer

SIGISMUND STOJOWSKI.

[January 1913]

While I sit at my desk, my eyes fixed upon this Barcarolle, trying to collect my humble wits for the purpose of helping readers towards a more intimate acquaintance with it—the vision arises of the Master's leonine mask, so similar to that of Beethoven; it seems I see him frown, hear his groan of discontent. In his lifetime enthusiastic misses would drive him wild by their eagerness to play his barcarolles, while the world refused recognition to more ambitious achievements of his creative genius.

Posterity, carried away by the ever-swelling stream of novel production, also serving other gods than were his, did nothing to make up what was resented as an injustice. Performers shun his larger works, doctors decree his workmanship careless, his critical sense deficient. Yet *The Demon* on the stage, the *Ocean Symphony*, the D-minor Piano Concerto [No. 4] on the concert platform assert their right to existence. And young ladies still play his barcarolles. There is justice at least in that tribute of the *vox populi* to a certain quality of inspiration. His nature was spontaneous, ardent, exuberant, passionate. His impresario and friend, Hermann Wolff [1845-1902], tells us that every thought had to find immediate expression and he was continually bubbling over with ideas. So it happened that many a short masterpiece jumped, like Minerva out of Jupiter's head, all armed for the battle of life perennial—while flashes of genius could not redeem the lack of patient toil, the price of vitality in any big work.

Melody is, in music, the most unconscious vehicle of spontaneous feeling; so, again, Rubinstein was a great melodist. No less a critic than R. Schumann in speaking of Rubinstein's Opus 1, states that the marked tendency towards melody was a fine promise of the boy's comprehension of music's true essence. When, as a mature artist, Rubinstein expressed his views on art, he refused to pass condemnation on Italian opera, because it was full of melodies. His own melody flows easy and abundant, rising to eloquence and pathos, also sinking into sentimentality and emphasis. From the treasury of Slavic folk-song he seldom drew, finding inspiration in the subjective elements of his own rich temperament. In spirit he was a romantic, imbued with German culture and classical traditions. An affinity exists between Rubinstein and Schubert, whom Rubinstein adored. At times, behind some turn or figure, the aristocratic features of Chopin, the "piano-bard" of whom he so eloquently spoke, arise in Rubinstein's works. But the affiliation is most direct with Mendelssohn. Rubinstein was a far less perfect, more intense and fiery, vehement and dramatic Mendelssohn.

Life's vicissitudes affected him for the most part externally; his art bears throughout the leading features of a strong personality, whose evolution did not undergo sharply diversified phases. Towards the end he grew ever more conservative and academic. He started revising his youthful works in that spirit, unfortunately it happens, to their evident damage. As a virtuoso he stood unrivalled at his day—the Titan of the keyboard. But from a life's habit of addressing and commanding crowds, his music became permeated with a certain striving for effect. His piano style is simple, comparatively uninteresting. It derives its effectiveness rather from tone-color—he possessed the command of a wonderfully rich tone—than from ingenious technical combinations such as those which pianists revel in. Simplicity was to him the highest aim of artistic endeavor; a high but dangerous goal, for simplicity implies absolute sincerity, and who but the very greatest ones can afford to be wholly outspoken without disclosing some vulgarity?

The Barcarolle, its Origin, Rhythm and Character

The water evidently fascinated Rubinstein. His first opus bears the title *Undine*, his greatest symphony that of *The Ocean*—and he wrote six barcarolles for piano. This name is derived from the Italian: *barca*, *barcajudo*—boat, boatman—and primarily designates a boatman's song. Subjective imagination, of course, substitutes for the boatman the creator's own personality with the world of his emotions. There is a wide gap between Mendelssohn's *Venetianisches Gondellied*—a remembrance of the *Gondolier of Venice*—and the immense tone-poem of Chopin's *Barcarolle* that seems to depict all water ever did, as well as all the feeling it ever aroused in man's breast. Rubinstein's barcarolles strike the medium; they are poetic little tone-pictures distinctly partaking of the *genre* origin.

The one in F, his first—it was published as Op. 30 jointly with an *Appassionata*—is built on two themes: the first one has an undercurrent of melancholy and pathos, suggestive of individual emotion and northern skies, whereas the second—that of the middle section—takes us right to Italy, with its sunshine, blue waters and gondoliers, seems to voice collective feelings, susceptible as it would be, of choral setting. Contrasted are their keys and rhythms; the somber F minor in graver 3/4 (9/8) time and serene F major in more vivid 6/8. It is the latter that brings the conventional cadence of the barcarolle, in which a stronger, sustained beat alternates with a weaker and shorter one, after the metric — ◡ — ◡ scheme corresponding to 6/8 time. The other rhythm—9/8 rather than 3/4, the quarter notes of this being almost constantly divided into three eighths— carries with it an extension of the cadence's downfall:

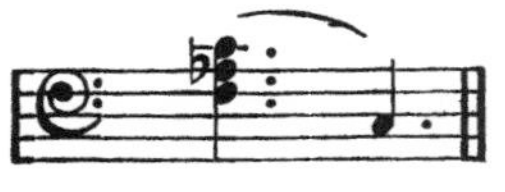 instead of as in 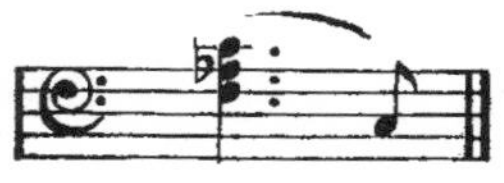

—the boat rolls up quicker than it descends from the top of the wave.

The Form: Analysis of its Elements

The structure of the piece proceeds from the so-called form of the minuet, in which a trio or middle section separates the first part from its repetition at the close. But the parts do not subdivide after the scheme of the dance-form. Two extended song-periods are juxtaposed and linked together, each of them remaining an undivided unit. Closer examination reveals that the first part consists of three sections (marked **A**, **B**, **C**). After four introductory measures, establishing the rhythm and harmonic foundation, the main theme (**A**) starts with a four measure phrase, that is the embryo out of which its entire melodic structure evolves. Measure 5—counting from **A**—is identical with m. 1; m. 6, rhythmically analogical with bar 2, introduces a modulation to the relative major key, leading to a perfect cadence in that key, the effect of which is ingeniously palliated by the fact that the high A♭ (**1**)—a surprise after the descending diatonic steps that precede—on which the new tonic is reached, also is the starting point of the phrase's return to the initial key.

Let us invariably adjust our interpretation to the architecture of the musical phrase. This entire exposition is to be played with full, rich tone, the fingers not too much curved, but rather lengthy on the keys, the wrist loose and low, to enable us to use the weight of the lower part of the hand to the best advantage in tone production.

The modulation to the more ardent key of A-flat demands an increase in dynamics; the natural dropping of the voice towards the cadence would lead to a *piano* effect on the high A♭ (**1**).

Harmonic Background: Development of the First Period

In studying the underlying harmony we notice—in this section and throughout the piece—that its bass moves but little. This conveys a sense of space and depth. The diatonic steps (**2**), can be brought out somewhat by sustaining and decreasing [tone], which brings an element of interest into the homophonic texture of the whole.

Back we are in F minor, and Section B starts by repeating the initial four measures for which we can now use a softer touch and which becomes adorned with turns and grace-notes. (In this, as in many other instances, the present writer prefers following the original edition, in which the utterance seems more simple, spontaneous and free than in the later revised one.)

Four measures after **B**—a new development of the phrase begins, rises passionately, modulating to the subdominant, then through the key of G- flat gets back to F minor, decreasing softly to conclude on the tonic. Time for the grace-notes (**3**) (**4**) should be taken-from the previous measure, so that the bass is struck with the sustained note following. They require a sort of ecstatic expression, the second one being held slightly longer and accented, also rigorously connected with the subsequent note.

The new member of the phrase is now partly repeated—compare mm. 4–7 with 12–15 after **B**—leading to a different expansion, in which the altered chord [French augmented sixth]:

alternates in measures with the harmony of the dominant, until it remains in suspense on the latter (**6**). The threefold repetition of this alternation lends itself to a gradual diminuendo, more logical than the sudden *p* marked on G♮ (**5**) and the *p* effect can thus be reached on the high C (**6**) (again after the first version).

The next two measures (**7**), totally disconnected melodically with what precedes and what follows, appear like a sudden obstacle in the course of the boat. Mr. Paderewski obtains a thrilling effect by playing those interpolated two notes *forte*.

The first part third section (**C**) is a coda, beginning with the first measure of the main theme again, which characteristic interval—after the phrase has flashed up once more and then resolved in imitative descending triplets (**8**)—becomes the connecting link with the middle section (**9**). The triplets mentioned must be played absolutely legato—the gliding of the fifth finger at (**8**) from the black to the white key will prove helpful—gradually decreasing and calming down. The vibrations on C (**10**) indicate the anxious rise of a new mood; their number is immaterial and could be augmented, the effect driven at being an accelerando and crescendo that then subside until the impatient rhythm ♪♫ ♫ gently melts into the placid ♩♪♩♪

The Middle Section Analysis and Performance

The B-flat major chord, on which the new subject (**D**) starts in, comes to us like a soft fresh breeze. It enters *pp*—the accompanying chords particularly subdued, while the sustained notes of the melody must be pressed down by the upper fingers for the purpose of producing a singing tone. *Legato* playing is also essential to this melody; fingers must skillfully creep above one another. (The fourth above the third, for instance, at **11**.) Breathing, however, is refreshing between the slurs and the occasional connection of the two eighths out of three (**12**), (**15**). Likewise the taking away of the last note of some measure (**13**), (**14**), add to the ever increasing vividness. For this entire section is a long, drawn-out climax; the period divides itself into phrases of eight bars, each starting identically, but each time intensified in harmony and color, until a buoyant *f*—rather *ff*—is reached (**16**). The *p* mark on the following perfect cadence (**17**) seems excessive, although there is a decrease in the descent of the melody in the previous measure. The fundamental F need only be played on the first beat (**17**), (**18**)—the pedal keeps it down and only the author's huge hand accounts for the useless but uncomfortable repetitions. These have been accordingly omitted in the present edition.

The octave-jump down from a sustained half note, which for the first time appears between mm. 3 and 4 of section **D**, now opens the closing phrase (**E**) of this middle part, a bridging over to the first subjects' return. The spirit of exuberance and joy becomes gradually repressed; like a protest the broken cadence on the D flat major chord violently rolls up (**20**); fragments of the passing away phrase then grow doleful and faint— while our attention has been startled by a new feature (**19**), a diverting announcement of things to come.

Third Part and Conclusion

Back we are to the element and its melancholy. An accompaniment of realistic charm is evolved above, suggestive of splashes in the water, while from the depths rises the voice of the initial theme (**F**). It is now played by the left hand; where the right helps out, the interchange must be inaudible. The melodic line must remain undisturbed. The chords on the first beat can be rolled; in the first edition they are written as grace-notes. The notes in parenthesis (**21–26**) are later additions, which the writer does not play, confining himself to the single bass-note of the early edition. The treatment of the pedal claims particular care and some skill in passages when the harmony requires a change of pedal, while at the same time the melody should suffer no interruption, the right hand must get hold of the tied over melodic note until the new pedal and the left hand, after having struck its bass-note, can come to the rescue of continuity of line [one after (**21**)]:

At (**23**) smoothness of execution can be facilitated by changing the right hand's D to F in the last beat of the previous measure—a change wholly immaterial— which secures the tied melodic note F in the way as above.

Pursuing our formal analysis to the end we find that in this third part—varied and shortened repetition of the first—the Section **B** is omitted. G corresponds to C—and brings the whole to a conclusion somewhat overburdened with harmonic "fillings" that take away from its loftiness. But as the editions published at the composer's lifetime here agree, reverence bids us to keep hands off, in spite of the Frenchman's saying, more true in art than anywhere: "the letter kills, the spirit vivifies."

BARCAROLLE

Edited by S.Stojowski

A. RUBINSTEIN, Op. 30, No.1

A Lesson Upon the Schubert-Liszt "Hark, Hark, the Lark"

By the distinguished Virtuoso, Teacher and Composer

SIGISMUND STOJOWSKI

[February 1914]

"My musical compositions are the product of my intellect and of my sorrows," Schubert wrote in his diary, and—remote as he then was from either happiness or fame—he remarks: "Those which were born of sorrow alone, appear to give the world the most satisfaction." But if many of his sad inspirations, whether born of personal grief or of the artist's sensitiveness to emotions felt and worded by poets, have ever stirred and moved fellow men, so does the world now also love to seek solace and uplift in another phase of his art, when he would in a happy frame of mind so natural to this child of Vienna, turn joy into beauty. Not *only* the pathetic *Erlking* of Goethe but *also* Shakespeare's joyous "Serenade" ["Morgenständchen," the source of "Hark, Hark" from *Cymbeline*, Act II, scene III] sing in all memories and quicken the hearts of good men "who have music" in themselves as assumed in the *Merchant of Venice*. It happened that the man who would, in moments of gloomy depression express the wish of never awaking the next day, has greeted in an immortal song the morning's rise with a gladness as luminous, a buoyancy as warm, a charm as irresistible as the summer morning itself flooded by sunshine.

How the Song was Written

The story of this song's conception (1826) testifies to Schubert's extraordinary facility as well as to the power of abstraction of which an artist's imagination may be capable. While turning the leaves of a book in a tavern in a Viennese suburb, he suddenly exclaimed: "I have a lovely melody in my head." A friend tendered a sheet on which he had traced some lines, and Schubert, in the midst of the company, and in spite of the noises around, jotted down the song. The result was "a wonderful, sweet air with admirable rich words to it," as is said in the second act of *Cymbeline*—a little musical gem born in "that mysterious borderland where the enthusiasm of the untutored and the admiration of the knowing ones can meet," which is Victor Hugo's definition of a masterpiece.

The Liszt Transcriptions:
Their Artistic and Educational Value

Among the knowing ones, who were soon to herald the greatness of Schubert to the crowd as yet ignorant of his message and meaning, was a master mind, the Titan of the keyboard—Franz Liszt. According to his own confession Schubert's songs would move him to tears. Introduced by Schubert's friend, the singer Vogl, these songs were just coming into prominence when Liszt undertook to contribute his own precious and considerable share towards popularizing and immortalizing them by the transcriptions he made for the joy and benefit of the piano-playing world. Endowed with a wonderful sensitiveness to beauty, with a heart vibrating with all the generous impulses of the truly artistic nature, Liszt became a pioneer for all the elder and younger brethren in art, and devoted to this noble mission not only his powers as an interpreter, but also a very special form of his creative genius.

Liszt not Merely a Transcriber

Some severe and scarcely dispassionate critics call Liszt merely a "transcriber;" others, more judiciously, name him a "collector of cultures" because of his astounding power of assimilation. Among many just and enlightened remarks contained in Mr. Busoni's otherwise debatable pamphlet, *New Æsthetics of Music* [1907], is the statement of the self-contradiction of those who at the same time despise and condemn all transcriptions, and admit and even admire the variations as an art form. One has, of course, to turn to such transcriptions as Liszt's to fully realize the similarity of the two proceedings. Ordinary arrangements for other instruments simply concerned with transferring the notes given with more or less accuracy and attempting playability through partial elimination or idiomatic treatment of the new medium by more or less appropriate changes in the context—though they occasionally may seem like respectable puzzles that were hard to solve, cannot claim the appellation of works of art, as the creative element does not enter into them. They may at their best be compared to photographs in which the lines have been preserved, but the color and life that were in the original are missing. Liszt's personality acted like a prism through which the ray of light would pass to get reverberated in hues manifold, novel and iridescent.

How Liszt Transformed the Thoughts of Others

His was the capacity of taking in another's thought so completely that he could render it transformed, adapted, recolored, vivified, as it were, by transfusion of new blood, in another raiment in which the garments would bear the unmistakable mark of his personality, while out of them the "Spirit" of the original would shine in immaculate beauty. The infallible tact with which Liszt would proceed in his treatment of a given subject in accordance with its character is truly illuminating. Now he would be content to approach the original in a faithful, though different instrumental setting, then again expand it into actual variations of his own. A comparison between the *Erlking* already mentioned, and the "Morgenständchen," under discussion, is indeed interesting. In the momentous drama of the first, Liszt merely reproduced and intensified pianistically the lines of an evolution in which every phase was marked by Schubert himself: while in the other song he took advantage of its light mood and of the recapitulation indicated by the composer to enrich his pianistic version of it with a delightful variation leading to a perfectly consistent and harmonious close of his own.

The Educational Value of the Transcriptions

From the educational standpoint these transcriptions of Schubert by Liszt have a very particular value. While most of them are technically accessible only to the advanced student, they may become a most helpful stimulus for artistic growth at that stage. The piano student concerned with the manifold problems of a complex and exacting technic is, indeed, too prone to develop what a conservatory director once contemptuously called a "piano mind." The fallacious magnetism of great means to conquer too often defeats the end, which is expression, by the very means which are technique. Nothing is more enlightening and stimulating to the young artist's imagination than reading the words of these songs previous to their study to the purpose of first entering into the intimate way in which the music is blended with the poetry, of realizing next how respectful and illustrative of every shade of expression Liszt's treatment is in all its richness and diversity. Such a study can not only awaken an imagination apt to be dormant or dulled by technicalities, but it also leads to the full and necessary comprehension that our fingertips can become just as expressive and eloquent vehicles of thought as are the words spoken by our lips. This is a basic fact in the pianist's artistry where the control of one's ear is to help the skill of adequate touch in carrying out every poetic intention of the mind. My eminent colleague and friend, Josef Hofmann, could testify that such was also the conviction of his master, Rubinstein—and a detailed analysis of the "Morgenständchen," will provide ample opportunity for instructive examples.

Interpretive Discussion: First Part

The introduction (**A**), consisting of eight bars, is Schubert's own, but it appears in Liszt's setting enriched and amplified, the chords being filled out, the characteristic rhythm of two sixteenths on the third beat (see mm. 1 and 5) being enforced by doubling so as to stretch out the harmony to the very top of the keyboard. (Small hand may omit the F, lowest note of the right hand chord at (**2**)). It seems, indeed, suggestive of the beating of the wings of the skylark, that "contemptor of the ground," as Shelley has it, of the bird's hopping up and down from branch to branch. The touch required has to be feather-light; the repeated notes to be played with a loose wrist quickly moving, while the arm stays quiet and the finger remains crisp and firm. The pianist's arms, not having the natural skill of the bird in moving about, [should secure] every change of position by swiftly carrying over the hands upon the chords to come in advance of the stroke. But also the lyric mood of the song is conveyed from the very start by melodic notes that require a slight stress, and to emphasize which the editor suggests the shadings and pedalings as indicated in mm. 3, 4 and 7. The sixth (**1**) which is the top of the first crescendo may be rolled, while the subsequent fingering permits ending up the melody quite legato.

At **B** the voice sets in, the song begins. The general shading remains *piano*—the song only gradually developing into a passionate appeal to the fair sleeping one—the relationship between melody and accompaniment should be carefully observed, the notes of the melody requiring a singing quality derived from longer pressure with the corresponding finger, while the accompaniment retains all its winged delicacy.

The correlation between the declamation of the words and the musical phrasing should be closely studied too; accented syllables should correspond to metrical accents in the music, and legato must be observed where breathing would obviously be out of place. An instance is at number (**3**), where the appoggiatura C must be played connected with its resolution B♭, as shown in the German word "aetherblau" in which the first syllable is accented, and an interruption through breathing after it would be utterly pernicious. (It must be remembered that the song has been composed to the German words.) In the next bar the correct declamation of the words, "Phoebus neu erweckt," invites a crescendo in the left hand to which the melody is entrusted, while the tumbling down right hand figure (**4**)—Liszt's addition—admits of no emphasis, retard or cadence-like treatment. Its difficulty may be overcome by some preparatory exercise of this kind: (The thumb quickly moving up and down, while the second and fourth finger sustain their notes. And the reverse.)

The musical structure of the phrase, in accordance with the punctuation of the verses, proceeds by groups of four bars, into which, the repetition of words at (**5**) brings a diversion, through the added two bars that modulate to the key of the dominant.

The differentiation at (**5**) between the accented melodic notes [on beats one and four], and the accompanying chord in which the same key is struck [one sixteenth later in each case], should be minded—[and played] not with stiffness, but with a consciousness that does not exclude grace from the performance.

The following section **C** brings in—through the medium of the harmonic connecting note F—a distant key, that of G♭ of a deeper and darker hue in a truly Schubertian way. Its function is to prepare a fresh and striking return to the initial key by means of a wonderfully warm and expressive climax. Careful gradation is necessary, and this even permits of a *piano* effect on the words, "reizend" and "steh auf," when they occur for the first time (**6**) (**7**).

Upon that last word—the little poem's climax and synthesis—Schubert dwells a while; the performer should beware of pianistic brutality in the *ff*, and always remember he is playing a song and serenade at that! The composer reminds him of it by gently concluding after the passionate outburst and insisting on the word "suesse" ("sweet" applied to the "lady," which in the English text is at that place (**8**))— to which special emphasis is due, the seeming incorrectness of the phrasing prescribed suiting the poetic purpose here. That a broadening of the tempo matches the whole anticlimax and ending of the phrase need scarcely be insisted upon.

The Liszt Variation and Conclusion

As in many instances of simple song form—yet in harmony with the purpose of a serenade—Schubert helped himself out of the shortness of the piece by mere recapitulation. Liszt's creative bent and keen insight made him realize that at the piano this would not do. And so in the place of repetition he gave an exquisite variation of the figuration type (**D**). The harmonic structure underlying the original remains untouched, and the notes of the melody are maintained even if seemingly submerged by the embroidering parts (**9**) (**10**), or displaced (**11**). The running figures have for the most part to be played legato; an occasional staccato will sound refreshing, however, as for instance at (**12**), where it may bring a diversion, an added interest to the chromatic imitations in which the polyphony charmingly indulges.

Repetition had in olden days been a merely formal feature used at times by composers without much discrimination. In music of the romantic and modern type it becomes a means of expression; being either a fading echo of things previously uttered, or their more or less emphatic restatement. It is in the sense of enhancing the expression that Schubert mostly uses repetition of words. The variation which replaces repetition in Liszt's version is treated in the same spirit, the richer setting requiring an intensified rendition. The crescendo at (**13**) must be exuberant, and that very exuberance leads on to an amplification of the perfect cadence in F major (**14**).

But ere the second strophe of the song (**E** corresponding to **C**) appears in turn in its new garment, poise and calm have to be restored; the rit. and dim. have to be great, and even the hold proposed by the editor on the last F of the last bar before **E**—with a special change of the pedal during it—seems quite desirable.

After the entire nature had seemed to wake up triumphantly, soft breezes will join in the morning concert to the lady sweet. The performance of the suggestive little runs is anything but comfortable. Based upon the passing of the thumb, the difficulty of arpeggio—technic must be overcome by preparatory exercises of the type previously indicated at (**4**), also of the following order:

which can be extended thus:

and should be practiced slowly and repeatedly, applied to every single arpeggio. These may even be beneficially transposed half a tone higher (while retaining the awkward fingering of the original key).

An Effective Climax

The climax which ensues has to be shaded and graded in the way discussed above, with ever increased buoyancy. The doubling of the melody in octaves seems to the writer imperative (as indicated by the small notes below at (**15**) (**16**)).

At **F** begins an anticlimax and conclusion that are of Liszt's invention. The changes of position of the chords have to be secured—also in the previous section at (**17**) and following bars—by preparation, which is half the battle won in mastering the technic of skips.

The third bar from **F** must be considerably softened and broadened; the crossing of the hands at (**18**) gives a peculiar coloring and should be respected. In the next bar a little dynamic swelling seems desirable. Mr. Paderewski plays instead of the following arpeggio an exquisite little run derived from the rhythmical feature of the repeated sixteenths—it would be trespassing upon my rights to publish it here, however, even if I could wholly trust my ear and memory. In the last two bars the happy lark seems to be vanishing out of sight into the ether blue.

Revealing the Composer's Hidden Meaning
[September 1911]

It is difficult for some people who are not versed in the intricate mysteries of the art of music to realize how limited are the means afforded the composer for communicating to the interpreter some slight indication of the ideal he had in mind when writing the composition. The very signs with which the composer is provided to help him put his thoughts down on paper are in themselves inadequate to serve as a means of recording more than a shadow of his masterpiece as it was originally conceived.

Of course, we are speaking now in a large sense—we are imagining that the composer is a Beethoven with an immortal message to convey to posterity. In all these things Beethoven was obliged to adhere to the conventions adopted by others for this purpose of attempting to make the composer's meaning clearer to other minds. These conventions, like all conventions, are partly insufficient to convey the full idea of the composer, and partly arbitrary, in that they do not give the interpreter adequate latitude to introduce his own ideas in expression. The student should seek to break the veil of conventions provided by notation and seek a clearer insight into the composer's individuality as expressed in his compositions. From this point of view the so-called subjective interpretation seems the only legitimate one. In fact, the ones who pretend to be objective in the sense of being literal and playing strictly according to the marks of expression and admitting little elasticity in the interpretation of these are also, as Rubinstein pointed out, subjective at heart. This may be more concisely expressed thus: Since all things of permanent value in music have proceeded from a fervid artistic imagination, they should be interpreted with the continual employment of the performer's imagination.

On the other hand, the subjective method, right as it is in principle, can become, of course, according to the Italian saying, "Tradutorre, traditorre"—[see also p. 79] that is, an absolute treachery to the composer's ideal, if the performer's understanding and execution of the composition is not based upon long and careful investigation of all the fundamental laws and associated branches of musical study, which are designed to give him a basis for forming his own opinions upon the best method of interpreting the composition. Inadequate training in this respect is the Chinese Wall which surrounds the composer's hidden meaning. This wall must be torn down, brick by brick, stone by stone, in the manner in which the student may gain entrance to the sacred city of the elect, to whom the ideal of the composer has been revealed.

In a certain sense the interpreter is a cooperator with the composer, or, more definitely expressed, he is the "continuer" along the line of the musical thought and its adequate expression. Music, of all arts, is the unfinished art. When Bach, Beethoven, Chopin and Brahms put their thoughts down upon paper they left a record in ink and paper that must be born again every time it is brought to the minds of men. This rebirth is the very essence of all that is best in interpretive skill.

There is in all compositions a divine part and also a conscious part. The divine part is the inspiration. The conscious part has to do with dressing the inspiration in its most appropriate harmonic, polyphonic and rhythmic garments. These garments are the raiment in which the inspiration will be viewed by future generations. It is often by these garments that they will be judged. If the garments are awkward, inappropriate and ill-fitting, a beautiful interpretation of the composer's ideal will be impossible. Nevertheless, it is the performer's duty in each case to try to see through these unbecoming garments and divine the composer's thought, according to the interpreter's best understanding.

HARK! HARK! THE LARK.

MORGENSTÄNDCHEN
(Shakespeare)
FRANZ SCHUBERT

Edited by S. Stojowski

Transcription by
FRANZ LISZT

Lessons on Famous Masterpieces by Distinguished Virtuoso Teachers

Schubert's "Moment Musical" in F-Minor

by the Eminent Virtuoso Teacher and Composer
SIGISMUND STOJOWSKI.

[April 1913]

To the lover of nature one single tree rising towards the azure sky while the sunbeams play across its branches, or even a tiny solitary flower, bathed in heavenly dew, may give the keenest, purest pleasure, a sense of complete and absolute enjoyment. So can a fully satisfying aesthetic emotion be derived from a small canvas, in which the color-scheme is truly expressive, from a short lyric, charged with human thought, a little piece of music, perfect in its beauty within its humble scope.

Of such quality are many of Schubert's truest inspirations, and a parallel drawn from nature indeed seems apposite in his case for many a reason. His creative genius was like nature herself in her freedom, spontaneity and unconsciousness, in the lusciousness of her indiscriminating profusion. This music smells of the meadows where fragrant blossoms grow among weeds—(critics have dwelt upon his incapacity of sifting his thoughts almost to the point of obscuring his true and great significance in the evolution of the art of music)—and he seemed like a part of nature himself, in his childlike simplicity, his birdlike joy in song incessant! Unknown to him were the Promethean pangs of a Beethoven, nor did, within him, genius resemble the relentlessly gnawing vulture.

It seems as if Beethoven and Schubert had divided between themselves the task of founding modern music, taking the word "modern" in its spiritual and richer sense, suggestive of that world of individual emotions out of which our art has been made ever since, and regardless of conventional classifications according to mere patterns and of the much debated, never explained and ever artificial differentiation between "classics" and "romantics."

To Beethoven succumbed the part of forcing his titanic spirit into what Dr. Perry so excellently calls "the perfect balance between expression and design"—which is, by the way, the very definition of all classicism. Schubert, on the contrary, always remained the Aeolian harp, ever sensitive, instantly responsive to any vibration, and so became the forerunner of all that coming romanticism was to contain of subjective intimacy, of immediate and direct appeal to the heart.

Overshadowed by the immense figure of Beethoven in his lifetime, while living, obscure, in that same city of Vienna, Schubert is up to now often underrated in his historical importance. The wonderful but obtrusive thing called culture, mother of progress—and prejudice—has accustomed us to most highly—and righteously—valuing the wide intellectual grasp, the self-mastery and power shown by the human spirit in the conscious and controlled effort of vast constructions, but also, to at times confuse bigness with dimension. And we almost forget that, like the little flower, the solitary tree in Nature, so does artistic inspiration, cast into a small form, illustrate and reveal the mysterious and divine principle of all creation.

That Schubert's natural gifts and intuitive ways should have made him impatient of the constraint of larger forms, that he was born to become the true founder of artistic song, and felt impelled to transplant that flower of emotion into the field of instrumental music, lies at hand, although we must remember that all we hold of him is the legacy of mere youth. Others have explained—and excellently—wherein lies the greatness of these songs, direct embodiment of the poetical idea underlying—as tuneful as they were full of tunes. His piano-music, too, is saturated with rich melody: his best pieces derive

from song both form and contents, characterized as these are by the convergence of all the elements employed, such as melody, harmony, color, instrumental setting and structure, towards that one end so precious in song which painters have taught us to call atmosphere.

This tone-poet fond of playing on the heart-strings—a French writer calls him "the most poetic musician that ever was," while an American critic declares him the "most lovable of all"—shares with a newly enthroned instrument, the piano, fit companion of home and ideal confident of the musician's heart, the wonderful privilege of the intimate quality. Owing to this kinship it only seems amazing that in Schubert's enormous production the piano-lyrics should be but few: two sets of so-called *impromptus* and the "musical moments," outside, of course, of his endeavors in the sonata form and innumerable dances and marches. Yet few as they are, their aesthetic and historical value is of great import. While they do not increase the technical resources of piano style—Schubert's music is generally free from virtuosity—they are, in the highest sense of the word, idiomatic: they convincingly assert the superiority of the new instrument in its fine capacity for song and color. As compositions they stand out as novelties and models: independent little tone-poems, alone for their own sake, not cast into the mould of the current and ruling sonata form—"not chips from a great workshop," as Mr. [William H.] Hadow has it [1859-1937. See also p.78]. And the whole romantic future will indeed be tributary along that line of creative thought, from Mendelssohn and Schumann, Schubert's great admirers and discoverers, down to Johannes Brahms and the present day.

The "Musical Moments."

No biographical data can give us information on these "closely wrought miniatures" concerning their origin and meaning. We just know they appeared in print as Op. 94, with the first set of *Impromptus* (Op. 142), in 1828, the very year of Schubert's death. The most recent of Schubert's German biographers, Walter Dehns, asserts the manuscript bears the date December, 1827. Opus numbers are quite misleading where there are so many of them—and so is "inner evidence" in the case of one who turned out so many a masterpiece before even reaching maturity. Yet historians divide Schubert's activity into two periods, marked by the year 1818: that of youthful formation in which the influences of Mozart and Beethoven, the two older masters of the Viennese school, are more or less pronounced—and that of fully achieved and developed originality and mastery. Sir C[harles] Grove has assigned the piano lyrics to the latter period.

The "Musical Moments" differ widely from each other in style, form and character. Dr. [Oscar] Bie [1864-1938] finds fun detecting now and then a feature of the coming Schumann, while the face of old Bach, the eternal ancestor of all music, isn't altogether absent (in the prelude-like No. 5). The writer feels in No. 2 a suggestion of a Chopin Nocturne and No. 3, with which we are now specially concerned, seems to point to Brahms and his *intermezzi*.

Moment Musical No. 3

It is a delightful little dance, absolutely different from all dance-music written before, not only by Mozart and Beethoven, but also by Schubert himself. Schubert created in this "[Musical] Moment" a new, quite independent, unique specimen of dance, charged to the brim with a peculiarly woeful expression, yet so light, refined and fragrant that it seems conceived for some spirits fraternal to Ariel.

The delineation of character which precedes should convey to the performer that perfection will here be primarily dependent upon the quality of touch employed. It should be both light and singing, for we are struck at first glance by the alliance of tuneful melody with graceful rhythmical design. The persistent staccato of the accompaniment should be handled with extreme delicacy. Even in *forte* passages we should never forget the intimate quality of the inspiration. And as color—expressive but subdued color—seems the main thing in this little piece, the pedal must be used only with the utmost reserve, never blurring the clear-cut outline, but adding to the expression as a dynamic agent.

The structure, wonderfully harmonious in its simplicity, again shows the dual combination of song and dance. The first phrase (**A**) starts in with a very definite rhythmical design of the melody in the two first measures—an ever recurrent nucleus—which is supremely illustrative of Schubert's manner, as contrasted with, for instance, Mozart's melody-building, characterized by fluency rather than precision and definiteness of outline. Let us, in playing, emphasize the rhythmical precision by slightly accenting and gracefully taking off the short note after the grace-note [A♭, one measure before] (**1**) and lending some stress and a singing quality to the two sustained quarter notes [at (**1**)]. Three times is this rhythmical feature repeated—with a slight and welcome change the third time: ♪♪ 𝄽 ♩ instead of ♩ ♩ (**2**)—the repetition on ascending intervals implying a crescendo—not to be overdone, however! The last two measures of the phrase bring a decrease and conclusion on the tonic. The entire setting of this and the following melodic phrases is peculiarly Schubertian, too, in a certain "popular" quality, quite familiar in folk music, and which one is not surprised to meet with even in a most highly refined artwork of this naïve child of the Viennese people. There is no polyphony in the contrapuntal sense, but the melody is constantly coupled with harmonic and consonant filling notes, such as thirds, sixths, etc. These create some technical difficulty to the performer. At (**3**) the writer would suggest the following facility:

etc.

If, however, the original way be preferred, the F in the first chord of the bass should be omitted, thus:

The phrases B, and C, constructed in response to each other, both ending in the relative major key, form a sort of "trio" or middle section. The major mode brings a ray of sunshine; yet the tender melody sounds almost sadder than anything, just like in some Dutch pictures dealing with simple lives and their modest homes, the pathos lies in the light projected. Peculiar longing vibrates in the sustained dissonance at (**5**); it should be somewhat emphasized by the pressure of the finger, while the following resolution must recede in tone

quality. The pedal-mark is an instance of use of the pedal for a merely expressive purpose. A certain freedom may be permitted in the performance of this entire section. While slightly holding back the tempo at the start of (**B**), we should endeavor in changing the finger on the repeated keys, to get a sort of legato on the spot, conducive to a longingly singing quality of tone. It may be noticed that the repeated quarter-notes by which the new phrase sets in—also other details such as the short eighth preceded by a grace-note—directly derive from the context of the initial phrase. Schubert instinctively found a device of unification of material, which the cleverness of a Brahms is going to exploit to the point of leaving no stone of a foundation unturned in its logical development. The endings of both phrases of this section are noteworthy, too. In that of (**B**), the melody's accompanying *alter ego*, the lower voice, is called upon to step into the foreground—at (**6**)—while the upper voice now fills out the harmony and stays in suspense on the dominant prolonged into the fifth of the tonic. Owing to this, the cadence of the responding phrase (**C**), in the same key retains its freshness and acquires more finality: the tonic now being on top. The sixths of this ending (**8**) disclose an instructive point from the instrumental point of view. A technical deficiency—the difficulty of absolute legato in the playing of double-notes—turns into an advantage to interpretation: strict legato, applied only to the upper part, asserts its melodic supremacy. That this lies in the composer's intention, is revealed by the need he felt in tying over the first of the two grace-notes at the very beginning (**1**)—so that the melodic note C stands out, being struck alone. It may be mentioned here, although this seems obvious, that all grace-notes are played before the beat. The initial phrase can now be repeated (**D**) with an even more feathery touch than at the outset. The extension (**E**), leads over to the coda (**F**), and is particularly illustrative of some of Schubert's harmonic devices, such as the alternation of minor and major mode (**10, 12**) —a play which Brahms, again, is going to exploit. The bold B♭ against the B♮ of the bass (**11**), is a fine instance of what [Mathias] Lussy [1828-1910] calls the "pathetic accent:" when repeated it can be singled out not by accenting, but by subduing and, possibly, by softly rolling the two notes:

The lingering over the 6/4 chord of the major key (**12**) followed by the dominant ninth (**13**), is a gradual working up toward light, in which inner exuberance is held back, as it is in the whole coda, by outward restraint. Simply peaceful should be the close of this dainty little thing that expires its breath. The harmonic "finesses" (**14, 15**) must be slightly marked, for all harmonic devices in Schubert's music have an expressive meaning. The discrimination and aesthetic instinct shown in the use of harmony, and especially dissonance by this genuine innovator, might serve as a warning to some modern writers who fail to realize that excess is a lack and a danger and it seems as if one could hear the voice of this high lord in the realm of our art, crying out from beyond the grave, to all of us: *caveant consules*.

MOMENT MUSICAL

Edited by S. Stojowski

F. SCHUBERT, Op. 94, No. 3

A Master Lesson on Schumann's "Novellette in F"

By the Eminent American Composer-Pianist

ARTHUR FOOTE

[October 1928]

Robert Schumann, the creator of so many beautiful things in his short life (1810-1856), was a contemporary of an extraordinary number of famous composers. In 1815, Beethoven, Schubert and Weber were still living. Berlioz was but a few years old; while there were also Mendelssohn (1809), Chopin (1810), Liszt (1811), Verdi (1813) and Wagner (1813). The Romantic period in music art and literature was beginning and emotion was sought for self-expression; so that great would have been the surprise of these men had they been told that a century later distinguished composers avowedly aimed at writing music from which emotion and romance should be excluded, their place being taken by technical ability (for this is what "central" music means.)

With all composers whose work has endured (remember that the *Fantaisie* Op. 17, is ninety years old), it is in their music that they speak to us. At the same time, a knowledge of Schumann, the man, and of his curiously imaginative, self-absorbed nature, expressing himself only in his music, helps us to understand better what he wrote. For one who plays him it is well worth while to read a good account of his life, such as is found in Grove's Dictionary of Music.

One way by which a composer can justify his claim to a place with the elect is by so writing as to influence the development of music. This may be expressed in form (as did Mozart and Haydn with the Sonata, Liszt through his invention of the Symphony Poem); through counterpoint (as by J. S. Bach); by harmonic innovations, as those of Liszt, Wagner and Franck, and by the breaking of other new paths. With Schumann it was by his manner of writing for the piano that he did something new, influencing composers who have came after him. It had come to be felt that the plain scale and arpeggio, the most natural technical material for the piano, were beginning to be worn pretty threadbare. The much greater, as well as more supple and artistic, employment of the pedal necessitated by the compositions of Chopin and Liszt, was also an important factor in the change that was coming. These composers were leaving the well-trodden ways and exploring new paths, putting fresh life and interest into piano technic.

Schumann practically gave up the old plain scale and arpeggio. In the *Kreisleriana*, for example, there is not a single scale, nor are there any arpeggios of a purely ornamental nature. He was an experimenter at the keyboard, at least during the earlier years—often with success, sometimes not. In the preface to his *Paganini Studies* we can see how interested he was in working out technical problems.

His writing was often such as to demand an excessive use of the damper pedal, and one cannot help wondering whether he was sensitive to the unclear effect sometimes resulting. It is a curious thing that both he (in the ending of his *Papillons*) and Liszt (in the D-flat *Consolation*) almost seem to have foreseen the sostenuto pedal.

Novellette in F

In this *Novellette* the general direction, "In a marked and forcible manner," although indefinite as to tempo, does imply moderation as to speed. The metronome mark suggested (♩ = 88) is slower than that found in many editions, corresponding with the *Tempo Ordinario* of

Handel, used by him as an indication of comfortable and moderate speed in many of his choruses. The second section (mm. 21–48) calls for more animation and elasticity (so that ♩ = 96–104 is suggested); while, on the other hand, as the section in D-flat major, to be interesting, must be played very expressively, a return to a slower tempo is advised.

As to the construction of the piece, the rondo form is followed, though, to be sure, but a fragment of the first theme is given in mm. 82–85. Schumann was evidently fond of this form, as is shown in his *Arabeske*, Op. 18, although [rondo form] already had fallen out of favor with composers. He, indeed, carried its principles so far as in one case to build a rather unwieldy structure, in the *Faschingsschwank aus Wien*, in which the themes come as follows: A, B, A, C, A, D, A, E, F, A while in *Blumenstück*, Op. 19, we have a piece that oddly gives the impression of a Rondo, not being one— the themes occurring: A, B, C, B, D, E, B, D, B.

As to the pedal in mm. 1-20 of this *Novellette*, while not necessarily with the chords, many players will prefer to use it. If so, it must not be put down after the beat (thereby connecting the chords in a legato) but at the exact moment when the chord is played, being held no longer than an eighth note. The reasons for its use in mm. 5 and 6, as in similar cases, are easily seen. In mm. 17–20, the omission of staccato marks being clearly intentional, the pedal may well be kept down a shade longer, although it must not connect the chords.

As to the staccato marks, we must remember that even by Schumann's time composers had ceased to define the ordinary staccato by two different marks (as to which Beethoven, for instance, was very exacting), the degree of shortness being really left to the taste and judgment of the player. We may be somewhat guided by the fact that, whereas in *p* any degree of staccato results in a musical sound, a very crisp one is, in *f*, *ff* or *sfz*, pretty sure to be harsh and unpleasant. The first measure might be accurately written:

The chords *must not be struck from a distance*, being best played with arm-touch. Let the fingers be at the surface of the keys before depressing them. The octaves should be played with a slight wrist action.

The triplets (as in m. 1), and especially those in passages such as occur in m. 6, should never be hurried (a common fault); while we must be sure that the 32nd note in m. 6 is played after the last note of the triplet. The first note of the triplet group must have its full value. In mm. 1–4, do not anticipate the climax of the mounting phrase by beginning the crescendo with too much tone. We should always be thoughtful as to this point, remembering that crescendo means that we are to have more tone *later*, but not at the spot where the mark is printed; just as with ritardando we merely *begin* to play more slowly by degrees. All such marks (dim., accel., and so on), imply a continuous, carefully graded progression—never interrupted by a return to the speed or amount of tone with which we started—and lasting until the end is indicated by some mark.

In m. 5, observe the *sf* and feel and express the natural < > of m. 6. Since the only dynamic marks here are *sf*, *f*, *ff*, <, especial pains must be taken to avoid monotony by getting as much shading in tone as is consistent with the marking.

The second section (21–48) is very different in character, a strong contrast being produced by the legato of the singing melody, as well as by the change to a *p* and the slightly faster tempo. The melody is of a certain monotony as to structure, being consistently composed of strongly marked two measure groups which always seem to demand the same treatment (< >), have little variety rhythmically, and end persistently in cadences. It is hard to make them overlap so as to produce a long melodic line. Much dynamic shading is demanded, care being taken that each phrase begins softly enough to have an expressive < >, as also that it ends with sufficient deliberation (*not rit.*) to avoid the appearance of hurrying into the next one.

In m. 22 the sixteenth note (which is also one of the triplet notes) is incorrectly written, as the passage ought to read:

while in m. 48 (two notes against three) the G comes halfway between E and B♭. This point is cleverly made clear in an Etude of Saint-Saëns (Op. 52, No. 4):

The turn in m. 34 is best played:

For mm. 45–46 a *pp* is welcome (perhaps with soft pedal) as well as a ritardando, which last is best prepared by a very slight expressivo in the measure before.

While every player should have the habit of obtaining a legato with the fingers (when this is possible), it is often the case that the pedal may well be added to obtain a more beautiful one, or that the pedal must be used when the desired smoothness cannot be got through the fingers; as in such conditions as the following:

In mm. 21–48 its use is practically continuous.

Legato often may be obtained (as here in many cases) by changing fingers on a note, as in m. 24. Organists are familiar with this device; but too many pianists have not made its acquaintance. The following exercise will be helpful:

Measures 61–81 are in strong contrast to the rest of the piece, the little motive of five notes being tossed, in polyphony, from one voice to another. A real problem is given us, for these short phrases must be made interesting to the hearer. Remember what Schumann says: *"Always play as if a master were listening."*

We have here an extreme case of his fondness for repetition of very short phrases, as also in the *Arabeske*, Op 18. This portion of the piece must be handled adroitly, for without elasticity in phrasing and lovely contrast in dynamics it easily becomes monotonous. As an instance, care must be taken that the accent marked for the first note of each group of five shall vary in intensity. The composer gives little help by his solitary *mf*. It is seldom that the player is so left to his own resources as here—"with great expression" might be written as our guide. After a hint of the first section (82–85) the second one returns, to be treated naturally, much as before. For the Coda (beginning at m. 125), a rather more animated tempo seems appropriate, with a slight slowing up for the last few measures; observe the brisk feeling that comes from the constant repetition of the triplets, in m. 123 to the end.

NOVELLETTE IN F

ROBERT SCHUMANN, Op. 21, No. 1
Composed in 1838

A Lesson Analysis of Schumann's Träumerei

By CLAYTON JOHNS

Professor of Pianoforte Playing, New England Conservatory

[April 1924]

In the days of Theodore Thomas [1835-1905] and his traveling orchestra, Schumann's *Träumerei* was one of Thomas' favorite small pieces, played with muted strings, or "sordini." Most violin students know about sordini, and most piano students *ought* to know about the so-called "soft pedal," by means of which in modern pianos the hammers are shoved over to two strings, instead of three, thereby producing a muffled tone.

In old times the pianoforte had only two strings for each tone, and one of the two strings, having been muted, the term of "una corda" (one string) had a real significance, but nowadays it is a misnomer, as the sign or term, instead of "una corda," should be "duo corde" (two strings). The old sign remains, but everybody understands, now, that "una corda" means the "soft-pedal," with two strings. Since a dreamy effect is produced by muted strings, there is no wonder that Mr. Thomas chose to place Schumann's *Träumerei* after a brilliant piece by way of contrast. Schumann never thought that his little piano piece would ever come to such glory; nevertheless, it still sheds glory to all music lovers all around the wide world.

Träumerei is only *one* of the *Kinderscenen* (Scenes of Childhood), but to play it *well* demands a high order of musicianship. Schumann loved to write dreamy music. In his sets of short movements, you generally find one or several dreamy ones among them. *Träumerei* is No. 7 of the *Kinderscenen*, and the author of this article quotes from a copy edited by Clara, the wife of Robert Schumann. The edition is therefore well authorized.

Let us now analyze this piece in detail hoping to bring out some of the beauties, and to lend a helping hand to a young student. To begin with, the piece is written in the key of F. If it were in G, or in E, the effect would be entirely different. The key of G, or E, is rather brilliant and high pitched in quality, where the key of F has a quieting influence, superinducing dreaminess. This, combined with the use of the "soft-pedal," establishes the proper setting.

The next step to be taken is to consider the quality of tone. Since it is taken for granted that *Träumerei* is a pleasant dream, the tone, therefore, should be pleasant; not having any real accent, only having pressure touch with fingers and wrists well relaxed, molding the form, not chiseling it. The Schumann edition has but one *p* mark, three ritards and five slight crescendos. The rest of the interpretation must be left to the musical instinct of the student.

Now, for a cut and dried analysis (neither Schumann nor his music was ever cut and dried). *Träumerei* is such a short piece; it is printed in full, and excepting for a little fingering and a little pedaling, the text conforms closely to Clara Schumann's edition.

The measures are numbered. The first eight measures are repeated, so the second part begins with m. 17. With m. 17 and the next seven measures, are all modulatory, with m. 25 the theme returns and continues to the end.

In the old order of things musical compositions were generally made up of sections and phrases, multiples of twos, fours and eights. Schumann often broke the rule, adding or subtracting one or more measures to or from a phrase; but in *Träumerei*, the phrase divisions are entirely "according to Hoyle." As you see, the thirty-two measures are strictly mathematical (four goes into thirty-two eight times). If you divide each phrase of four measures, you will find each subdivision, what is called a section; the first section of the two is something like a question, and the second section is something like the answer (only, "something like," because the real answer comes at the end of the piece). In *Träumerei* the first section ends [after] the third beat of the second measure, and the second section ends [after] the third beat of m. 4. Therefore each section begins on the fourth beat and ends on the third, thus completing the number of beats in each section or phrase.

Imaginary Breaths

If you take an imaginary breath at the end of the first section, you might place a comma after it. And after the second section, place a semicolon; another comma after the third section, often a colon after the fourth section, because the eighth measure ends on the dominant, so of course, the piece is only half done. In such a short piece there would be only *one* period, or full stop, and *that* one would be at the end.

With m. 17 the second part begins, like m. 1; but with m. 18 both melody and harmony set forth to explore new paths, but after exploring them, through m. 18, they come to a halt, harmonically, landing in G minor, at the beginning of m. 19. In mm. 19–20, the adventurer looks round to see what he can see in the way of variety until, with m. 21, he becomes more and more inquisitive and again looks round from a higher point of vantage in m. 22. Having seen a very different landscape and feeling a little tired, he decides to come down the hill, and returns home, m. 24, beat four. After his wanderings he is content to *remain* at home and apparently thinks there is no place like home, mm. 25–28. Compare mm. 25–28 with mm. 1–4. If, with m. 30, beat two, the traveler should ever be tempted to stray from his own fireside; after a pause, long enough to consider his mistake, he comes back for good and all, and never goes away again.

In all melodic compositions the melody is the chief thing. In *Träumerei* the melody must stand out and above the harmony, excepting the imitative passage, mm. 15–16, which becomes more prominent, with m. 17 the melody is resumed and continues through m. 18 until the next imitative passage comes, mm. 19–20. The next phrase of four measures, 21–24, is very much like mm. 17–20, only a little more progressive. Returning to the theme, with m. 25, the student can apply the melodic principles for himself to the last eight measures. The finality of the melody touch is very important, singing it, by pressing and relaxing the long notes, while the eighth notes should be relaxed or slightly tensioned, depending upon the increase or decrease of tone.

The Importance of the Bass

After the melody the bass is next in importance; therefore the bass in the first measure should have an uncommonly good tune as a foundation. The second beat of m. 2 begins with a grace note, but it must sound like a real bass note and be caught by the pedal; the rest of the chord should be relaxed and "rolled up" to the D, then pressed down. The first two measures of the bass are sufficient to give an idea of the rest of the piece. The inner voices should be more subdued than the melody and bass, excepting for the imitative measures, where each voice is given a chance to speak for itself. Be sure not to accent too strongly the chords in the right and left hands on the second beat of measure; and in similar measures give an extra pressure to them with a syncopated effect, but remember that they are harmonic, not melodic.

Thinking of phrase divisions: The first four measures are in the key of F. On the second beat of m. 4, the chord is *on* the fifth degree of the [tonic], not *in* the dominant. With m. 5, beginning with the second phrase, it repeats m. 1; but with the second beat of m. 6, a distinct modulation occurs, which adds a new interest, taking the first phrase *out* of the key and landing it on, and in, the dominant m. 8. The next eight measures are exactly like the first eight measures. With the first beat of m. 16, by reclaiming the B♮ on the first beat, the B♭ on the fourth beat returns to the original key F. Measure 17 starts again, hand in hand, like m. 1, but parts company immediately, springing into another key, entirely new, second beat of m. 18. This second beat is so inquisitive, it demands a solution of m. 18 and then, on the first beat of m. 19, it completely resolves itself, landing in a new key, G minor, wherein, mm. 19–20, it remains until m. 20. The second half of the fourth beat of m. 20 leads to a still newer key, m. 21.

Measure 21 is like m. 1, only in a different key. With the second beat of m. 22, it becomes "curiouser and curiouser" (inquisitiver and inquisitiver) as "Alice" would say, but by resolving down again to the fourth beat it begins to have an inkling of a return to the original key F. As mm. 23 and 24 are in the relative union of F, but in spite of the C♯, the C♮ brings it back to the tonic m. 25. From there on nothing happens until the second beat of m. 30, where after taking a long breath and refraining by a 6/4 chord (a most restful chord) on beat one, m. 31, it prepares through the fourth beat of m. 31 and the first beat of m. 32 for the final cadence on the second and third beats of m. 32.

Observe how much stronger the final cadence is compared to the other cadences, which are not conclusive, only leading up to something else which follows, while the final cadence leaves nothing more to be said.

Looking, again, over the whole piece. See how different the phrases are? The first four measures are melodic and harmonic, while in the second phrase of four measures 5–8, they are partly melodic and partly contrapuntal. The seventh and eighth measures are imitative; each figure of six notes must stand out above the harmony. Like many imitative phrases they are often in "threes." When Germany was a happy land there was an old German proverb which said, "All good things are in threes." This may or may not have anything to do with the case, but as a matter of fact most sequential phrases are in "threes." The next phrase, 17–20, is again partly melodic-harmonic and partly contrapuntal, also it is entirely melodically and harmonically progressive. The next phrase, 21–24, is still more progressive, that is, the melody and harmony must advance until it decides to return to the original key. All good music must be either progressive or retrogressive; never remaining in the musical doldrums. Having returned on the fourth beat of m. 24 the last eight measures are almost like the first eight measures excepting that the last four are more conclusive.

No Real Accent
It is difficult to give definite instructions about accent, as this little piece has no real accent; there is, of course, much rhythmic pressure and much relaxation, but accent in the ordinary sense of the term

would ruin any feeling of dreaminess; therefore press and immediately relax the long notes and relax or gradually tension the eighth notes depending upon the slight crescendos and diminuendos. The given marks for crescendo and diminuendo must be the general guide, but all printed marks are only suggestive and relative—never literal. In mm. 3–4 follow the directions for the short horizontal lines in the first and third beats of m. 3, and the first beat of m. 4. All the rest of the measures similarly marked should be treated in the same way. "Horizontal lines" mean a little more pressure.

There is little left to be said, beyond a word or two about fingering and pedaling. Finger according to the phrases and follow the phrase marks of Clara Schumann; doing that the student cannot go wrong. Over-edited pieces are usually misleading. Too many marks confuse the student. Instead of thinking of each mark, try to get at the heart of the piece, weighing it in the balance, then nothing will be found wanting.

Pedaling is a more difficult problem. The fundamental rules of pedaling are simple, but artistic pedaling is of a much higher grade, depending upon a wire spring, so to speak, in the ankle, wobbling it as it were, bringing out tones and overtones, and listening to each vibration, making the effect of a kaleidoscope. For the simple purposes of *Träumerei* the "harmonic pedal," added to the use of the "soft pedal," will be sufficient for the average student, if he will strictly follow the oblique pedal marks given for a few measures, as a sample. It goes without saying that a student must pedal harmonically, neither blur the notes nor begin nor end the phrase with a ragged edge.

It is too bad to have laid bare the bones and sinews of this beautiful little piece. It seems more or less like a musical vivisection. We are told that the suffering of a certain number of animate beings have to be endured for the general good. Let us hope the suffering of this acute analysis of *Träumerei* may lead some students to a clearer understanding of it. *Träumerei* is a sort of a "multum in parvo," like a perfect poem of two short stanzas by Heinrich Heine.

After all is said and done, unless the student considers the suggestions given above and applies them to his other studies the result will be hardly worth while. Once more: Remember the well known admonition, "Mark, learn and inwardly digest." That done the student will be ready to take up a "new piece" for study and, we hope, play it well.

TRÄUMEREI
REVERIE

R. SCHUMANN, Op. 15, No. 7

A Master Lesson on Senta's Ballad from Wagner's Opera "The Flying Dutchman"

Transcribed for the Piano by Franz Liszt

By Mark Hambourg

[December 1929]

Throughout history there have appeared at rare intervals men whose powers, whether they be of action or of creation, have exercised an extraordinary, even a cyclonic, effect upon the world in which they have lived. Such a man in the field of music was Richard Wagner, and it is to the credit of his great contemporary, Franz Liszt, that the latter was amongst the most enthusiastic friends and supporters of this rival talent. No shade or suspicion of jealousy seems to have ruffled the long friendship which knit together for many years these two Titans of music, and the rare sympathy and understanding which Wagner found in Liszt was a continual source of inspiration and of encouragement. Indeed, the opera house of the little town of Weimar, where Liszt lived for so long and made his own musically, was, together with Dresden, the first theater to perform the daringly original masterpieces of Wagner.

Liszt carried admiration of his friend's compositions so far as to transcribe most of them for his own instrument, the piano. Hence we have, amongst many others, the piece before us today, Liszt's transcription of the ballad of Senta, taken from Wagner's opera "The Flying Dutchman."

This early work of Wagner's was the second of his operas and was conceived during an eventful voyage which he took by sea from Riga to London in a sailing vessel in 1839. The opera was actually not committed to paper till two years later, in 1841, at Meudon in France, where Wagner spent the spring of that year. "The Flying Dutchman" marks the beginning of a new era in operatic music, as Wagner here throws away the ubiquitous vocal dexterities and spectacular scenic effects in fashion at that time on the operatic stage and endeavors rather to transfer to his music something of his own passionate feelings of poetical inspiration. Thus "The Flying Dutchman" became symbolical of the composer's personal sufferings at the moment, of his friendliness and his loneliness amongst strangers. Who could realize better than he the type required for his hero, who, doomed to roam unceasingly, longs vainly for rest and the redeeming love of a woman?

The Break

This necessity for self-expression led Wagner eventually to the breaking of the conventional operatic forms which were insufficient to contain the fervency of his imagination, and already in "The Flying Dutchman" this tendency is very apparent. Everyone knows the romantic legend of the "Flying Dutchman"—how he made an oath to sail around the Cape of Good Hope in the teeth of a storm even if he had to sail till doomsday, how the Devil heard his vow, accepted it and caused his fate to be that he should roam forever on the sea, far from his home and all he loved. Yet every seven years the Evil One allowed him to come ashore for one day, and if, during that time, he could find a woman who would love him enough to sacrifice herself for him, he would be saved from his doom.

The story is told in the opera in the beginning of the second act by the heroine, Senta, in a dramatic song in which she sings the whole account of the poor Flying Dutchman's fate to her girl friends who with their spinning wheels sit working around her. This song or ballad, as it is generally called, which Senta sings, is the subject of our piece here and is wonderfully transcribed from the operatic original by Liszt. In it is to be found the essence of the whole opera, the weird and restless atmosphere of the stormy Northern seas, the demoniacal, terrifying gloom which shrouds the mysterious Dutchman, and, gleaming through it all, the tenderness and pity of the love *motif* which Senta evolves, in her sacrifice and faithfulness unto death. This sacrifice which is foreshadowed in her song leads her to throw herself into the sea in the last act. Thus does she break the Devil's spell and takes her poor Flying Dutchman safely to his eternal rest.

Dark Prophecy

The ballad opens with a restless ominous motive full of foreboding. The eighth note on the first upbeat, $E\flat$ in the right hand, at the opening of the music should be made very exact in value, while the sixteenth note in a similar position at the end of m. 1 should sound also very strictly as a sixteenth of the measure, in contrast to the longer eighth note of the first upbeat. In m. 4, the last sixteenth note upbeat in the treble must be played with a quick wrist movement, to facilitate the passing of the fourth finger on to the fifth finger in the next measure, and this wrist movement should be repeated each time the figure occurs, up to m. 9. The piece, which starts *mezzo forte* in the first measure, dies away to *pianissimo* in the eighth measure with a long pause on the rests in m. 9. Then in m. 10 there begins a running figure in both hands conveying feelings of agitation and of rising storm. There should be a swelling of tone in m. 10, during this figure, from *piano* to *mezzo forte*, and then diminuendo again, to resume crescendo up to the culminating notes of the figure, D and $E\flat$, in the beginning of m. 12. After this the tone subsides once more into *piano*. The concluding note of the figure in the upper voice, namely $F\sharp$ on the first beat m. 14, ought to be taken by the left hand as an octave with the bass note, instead of by the right hand, as it is written in the music.

After the pause in m. 17, there appear single notes in the treble, eighth note D, on the last beat of m. 17, and G dotted quarter note on the first beat of m. 18. These notes are repeated three times in reiterated calls, until m. 22 is reached. These calls should sound as though played by a horn ringing out some kind of summons. Then on the last upbeat of m. 22, the ballad proper begins with the main narrative theme of Senta's song describing the gloomy plight of the Flying Dutchman. The first four notes of this song should be given with emphasis, and the next phrase starting on the last beat of m. 23 should be slightly slower in tempo. Then the narrative notes start again *a tempo*, and the pitying phrase in measure 26 which succeeds them must be rendered with much expression.

The Waves Interpolate

This part of the song is repeated, but in m. 31 a sinister atmosphere comes over the imagination of the story teller, and the restless heavings of the relentless sea appear to rumble and rage and interrupt the course of the narrative. The strident figures in the right hand in m. 31 should strike the ear with ferocity and a vivid accent be given on the diminished fifth on the fourth beat of this measure, whilst the summoning octaves in the left hand must be well brought out. The tone rises increasingly till it reaches sforzando and *double forte* in m. 33 where the octaves in the treble should sound like veritable blasts of the horn, and the chromatic octave scale in the bass like galloping horses (the wild horses of tempestuous "Boreas"). Louder and louder with gathering impetus the raging waves and storms of the unfortunate Dutchman's perpetual voyage seem to be conjured up by Senta's horror-struck vision, and the octave blasts in m. 37 become like those of trumpets heralding the approach of his haunted ship across the fury of the waters. In m. 37, also, these trumpet calls develop into a regular musical figure which continues up to the end of m. 42 and must be played very rhythmically.

At m. 46 the storm dies down, and after a long pause the second theme of Senta's song is introduced in m. 48 where she tells how every seven years the doomed sailor may come ashore for one day to seek a woman's true love, his only means of salvation. In the rendering of this inspired theme of love and compassion, the melody must be well brought out with tenderness and beautiful phrasing. In m. 50, the eighth note, D, on the third beat in the treble can be taken with the left hand instead of with the right, as it is printed, for this change of hands imparts more grace to the execution of the phrase. In m. 51 the hand should be lifted from the keyboard in the treble after the tied quarter note F on the first beat, before taking the sixteenth note G which follows it. This action will lighten the sound of the phrase and give the correct value to the sixteenth notes in time and in tone. Proceeding to m. 54, the first note in the measure, the quarter note, B, and the following eighth note, D, can also be taken with the left hand, for the same reason as is given in m. 42.

Senta's Prayer

The second main theme of pity is succeeded in m. 56 by a very beautiful development of melody in which Senta prays for the redemption of the Dutchman. At m. 62 this lovely prayer, breathing forth faith and hope, comes to a close, and the ominous calls of the bass horns are again heard very markedly in the left hand, but *piano*, as though in warning, and then with a crescendo up to m. 56, from whence the music returns to diminuendo. Coming to the end of m. 68 on the last upbeat, Senta's initial narrative theme is resumed with ornamentations, and here the notes of the song should predominate well over the running chromatic accompaniment in the left hand. The first two sixteenth notes of this figure in the lower voice should be taken by the right hand in conjunction with the fourth G and D in the treble, whilst accents should be given on the first notes of the sixteenth note passages in mm. 70 and 71. Continuing to m. 72, as in the end of m. 68, the two sixteenth notes in the lower part should be taken by the right hand.

From the end of m. 72 until the end of m. 101, the music is a repetition of what has already been noted, and must be performed in a similar spirit. Where the trumpet calls develop in m. 85, into a descending sequence of progressions, the chords, as in m. 39, must be made very rhythmical and fierce in expression. There is a D eighth note on the fifth beat in m. 95, in the treble which should be played by the left hand, and also D and F eighth notes on the third beat of the following measure. Arriving at m. 98, the melody is repeated *pianissimo*, and in the declamatory phrase in m. 99, the last three eighth notes, G, F and D, should be played by the right hand. The succeeding phrase, however, starting on B quarter note,

the first beat of m. 100, should be given to the left hand, for the varying change of hands helps to give more point and significance to the passages.

In m. 102 there arises an impassioned development of Senta's prayer for redemption of the "Doomed One," and this proceeds with ever advancing intensity, and with a slight broadening of tempo in mm. 108 and 109, leading up to a sort of breathless pause at the end of 109. This pause only tends to make a more overwhelming effect of the fervor of emotion which reaches its height in m. 110 where the octave passage comes crashing down in a perfect frenzy. Returning to m. 103, the two last eighth note octaves in this measure should be stressed, and going on to m. 112, the lower notes of the octaves here, which are written in the music for the right hand, are easier played by the left hand in octave with the bass notes.

The Pity Theme

Continuing to m. 114, the second principal theme (the one of "pity," as I call it) of Senta's song returns, and should be played proudly and slowly with great emphasis, until m. 117 is reached, when the music, gathering momentum as it again rises to excitement, should quicken its tempo, and the rhythmical figures which now reappear and which I have elsewhere likened to the summoning calls of brass instruments, should become more and more wildly turbulent as they reiterate their feverish appeals.

In m. 120 the melody again revives, and the tempo must slow down, only to get faster in m. 123, which is similar in spirit to 117. So also are the succeeding measures until we arrive at 126 where the song bursts forth in the key of E major (but in the original tempo) for a final enunciation and gathers into an apotheosis of the prayer for redemption in m. 130 which must be played more slowly and with great force of passion. In m. 134 there is a slight ritardando leading to an *a tempo* in m. 135, where in ever-intensifying excitement the music whirls us on till it reaches a tremendous climax of trumpet calls in m. 142 which must be performed very heavily and majestically, producing a spirit of exultation, of finality, of destiny fulfilled! Thus the piece is brought to a triumphant close: the sacrifice has been completed; the Flying Dutchman is redeemed and is born up with his devoted Senta into Paradise.

SENTA'S BALLAD
from "FLYING DUTCHMAN"
(RICHARD WAGNER)

Transcription by FRANZ LISZT